LOVE FIRST

"A no-nonsense approach to how to save someone you love from the ravages of addiction disease."

—William C. Moyers
President, Johnson Institute Foundation

"*Love First* is destined to become the new classic on internvention for alcoholism and drug addiction. The most comprehensive book available on the life-saving technique of intervention, *Love First* will save lives! A worthy successor to Vernon Johnson's *I'll Quit Tomorrow!*"

—Kathy Ketcham
Coauthor, *Beyond the Influence, Under the Influence,*
and *The Spirituality of Imperfection*

"A landmark book that gives families life-saving tools to help get a loved one into recovery. Bravo for this book that puts love first!"

—Jim Ramstad
United States Congressional Representative

"*Love First* provides the most detailed account yet of how intervention works. A significant contribution to intervention literature. An empowering antidote to the disease of addiction."

—William L. White
Author, *Slaying the Dragon:*
The History of Addiction Treatment and Recovery in America

A Hazelden Guidebook

LOVE FIRST

*A New Approach to Intervention
for Alcoholism and Drug Addiction*

JEFF JAY AND DEBRA JAY

with a foreword by George McGovern

 HAZELDEN®

Hazelden
Center City, Minnesota 55012-0176

1-800-328-0094
1-651-213-4590 (Fax)
www.hazelden.org

Library of Congress Cataloging-in-Publication Data

Jay, Jeff, 1954–
    Love first : a new approach to intervention for alcoholism and drug addic-
tion / Jeff Jay and Debra Jay ; with a foreword by George McGovern.
       p. cm. — (A Hazelden guidebook)
    Includes bibliographical references and index.
    ISBN 1-56838-521-8 (pbk.)
     1. Alcoholics—Family relationships. 2. Narcotic addicts—Family relation-
ships. 3. Alcoholics—Rehabilitation. 4. Narcotic addicts—Rehabilitation. I. Jay,
Debra, 1954– II. Title. III. Series.

HV5132 .J39 2000
362.29'286—dc21   00-044957

Author's note
All the stories in this book are based on actual experiences. The names and details
have been changed to protect the privacy of the people involved. In some cases, com-
posites have been created.

The Twelve Steps are reprinted with permission of Alcoholics Anonymous World
Services, Inc. (AAWS). Permission to reprint the Twelve Steps does not mean that
AAWS has reviewed or approved the contents of this publication, or that AAWS necessarily agrees with the views expressed herein. AA is a program of recovery from alcoholism *only*—use of the Twelve Steps in connection with programs and activities
which are patterned after AA, but which address other problems, does not imply
otherwise.

The Alcoholics Anonymous Preamble (on page 195) is reprinted with permission of
the A.A. Grapevine, Inc.

08 07 06 05 04   11 10 9 8 7

Cover design by David Spohn
Interior design by Donna Burch
Typesetting by Stanton Publication Services, Inc.

In memory of
Pauline Ann Eisele

and

Robert Janiga Jay
who live on in our hearts

Contents

Foreword

If one of my family members were an alcohol or other drug addict and were not seeking help to deal with his or her addiction, I would call Jeff and Debra Jay and say, "Help." I know them as admired and treasured friends. But I also know them as professionals with knowledge and experience, both wide and deep, of the complicated, treacherous, and costly disease of alcoholism, as well as of other addictions. I share the view of these authors that alcoholism is the most serious and destructive of our public health problems. My knowledge of and insight about the estimated twenty million alcoholics and two million other addicts in the United States were sketchy and limited prior to the death of my daughter Terry to alcoholism at Christmastime in 1994. That sad loss of a most promising and engaging young woman whom I loved deeply forced me to delve into the struggles and possible emancipation of addicts.

One of the most important and critical steps in the rescue of an alcoholic is the intervention. This is the well-planned, carefully structured process in which family members join in lovingly but firmly confronting the alcoholic with his or her illness and the necessity of beginning treatment. Frequently the addict's close friends or employer is involved in the intervention.

The Jays have carefully assembled the step-by-step process of constructing and carrying out a loving and effective intervention. In their lives and work, the authors have encountered many of the myths related to alcoholics and other addicts, some of them deeply ingrained in the minds of intelligent people. They patiently and convincingly refute each of these myths. They discuss the excuses frequently used by the addict to account for his or her need for alcohol or other drugs and why he or she does not need treatment.

Perhaps more to the point is the manner in which the Jays work through the mistaken views frequently held by an addict's family. During the years of Terry's drinking, with its frequently sad results, she did seek help in treatment, counseling, and Alcoholics Anonymous programs. But we were repeatedly told by well-meaning, supposedly informed friends that we would have to wait until Terry really "hit bottom." The trouble is that when she "hit bottom," she died.

Intervention is a way of erecting a "bottom" before such a tragedy occurs. This point is persuasively made by these authors. The pages that follow are going to save many addicts and their families from years of suffering, loss, and sorrow. This is a tough-love book that underscores the importance of love. It is a life-saving manual for those who would live and love so that others might live.

GEORGE MCGOVERN
American Embassy, Rome
March 8, 2000

(George McGovern is a former U.S. senator and a 1972 presidential nominee. He is now the U.S. ambassador to the United Nations Agencies on Food and Agriculture in Rome. He is the author of *Terry: My Daughter's Life-and-Death Struggle with Alcoholism*.)

Acknowledgments

The information in this book comes out of work with hundreds of alcoholics and drug addicts and the people who love them. Their struggles, courage, successes, and setbacks bring depth and relevance to this book. We thank each of these brave and wonderful souls for all they have taught us. A special thank-you to the three women who generously allowed us to reprint the letters they wrote from the interventions in their families.

We are particularly grateful to our editor Richard Solly for his invaluable insights, guidance, and encouragement. We greatly appreciate and thank George McGovern for writing the foreword to this book and for the many opportunities his support has given us. We'd also like to thank the following people for their much-needed contributions: Jerry Boriskin, Ph.D.; Michael Castranova; Carol Colleran; Robert Karp, M.D.; Lori Forseth Koneczny; Robert Niven, M.D.; and Becky Post. We thank our proofreader Nancy Solak for her good work and her good nature.

We'd like to thank our friends and family who have encouraged and supported us: Sara Jay Bayer; Arnie Eisele; Patricia Hitchcock; Philippe and Marta Malouf; Beth Loew; Fran Kovac; Corbett Reynolds; Carlyn Erickson; Greg and Chris Dodds; Nan Reynolds, R.N., M.S.W.; George Mann, M.D.; Jeffrey and Joy Spragens; George Ritchie, M.D.; and Mel Schulstadt.

We would also like to acknowledge a debt of gratitude to the late Vern Johnson, D.D., the father of modern intervention, and to the many people whose work in the field of addictions has contributed to the base of knowledge from which this book emanates.

Note to the Reader

Intervention is the most effective technique that families can use to help a loved one suffering from chemical dependency. It is also the most ignored. But just as CPR is often the first live-saving step in helping a heart attack victim, intervention is the most powerful step that a family can take to initiate the recovery process.

There are many common misconceptions about intervention. Some think it is an emotional ambush or an uncaring attack. But *Love First* demonstrates that intervention is a carefully planned process founded on love and honesty. Many people have heard about *tough love* where tough comes first; this book puts *love* first.

Through our work in intervention, we have found that love is a powerful force when confronting addiction. In the past, expressions of love were delegated to a few brief sentences during an intervention. We've learned that when we expand the role of love, it is love, rather than toughness, that first breaks through denial.

In this book, we have written about intervention in the real way that families experience it. We have organized the information in a step-by-step fashion, we guide you through every nuance of the process, and we answer the many questions that families ask. If someone you care about is suffering from alcohol or other drug problems, this book will clearly explain how to use love and honesty to give your addicted loved one the chance to reach out for help. Read this book thoroughly and share it with others who love the alcoholic.

SECTION

1

*Insights into Alcoholism
and Other Drug Addictions*

What Does It Take to Get an Alcoholic or Addict to Accept Help?

"I don't know much about this problem, but one thing I know is that you can't help an alcoholic until he's ready for help." We've heard this statement hundreds of times. We've even heard it from recovering alcoholics and addicts, counselors and doctors. You've probably heard it from people you know, and maybe you've said it yourself. It's the most unchallenged myth about addiction and the one that stops us from responding to a deadly and destructive disease. It leaves us standing at the sidelines while addiction runs through our families like a freight train.

When we say, "One thing I know is that you can't help an alcoholic until he's ready for help," what we're silently thinking is: "Therefore, there's nothing you or I or anybody else can do about this problem." This is simply not true.

Take a look at what happens when we challenge this myth with a well-placed question: "If alcoholics and addicts won't accept help until they're ready, what will it take to get them ready?" When you ask yourself this question—*what will it take?*—you change the way you think about the problem and, in turn, change how you approach the problem. Can you remain resigned to the idea that there is nothing anybody can do, or does this question propel you to search out an answer? As James Allen reminds us in his book *As a Man Thinketh,* "Let a man radically alter his thoughts, and he will be astonished at the rapid transformation it will effect in the material conditions of his life."

Alcoholics and addicts get help not because they see the light, but because they feel the heat. Something comes along that shakes them up so sufficiently, they'd rather accept help than continue drinking and drugging. We call this shake-up *intervention*. Most intervention is an unorganized, grueling jumble of personal tragedy for the alcoholic and the family—divorce, job loss, financial ruin, domestic violence, child neglect, jail, cirrhosis, insanity, and, ultimately, death. Something tragic intervenes before the alcoholic or addict seeks recovery. However, intervention can be an organized, loving act performed by friends and family. One type of intervention takes years and years of suffering; the other, a few weeks of planning.

The reasoning behind the widely repeated phrase *hitting bottom* is that we must wait for negative consequences to overrun the alcoholic or addict's life before he will accept help. Prior to the development of intervention techniques in the 1960s by Dr. Vernon Johnson, families had no other recourse than to wait for the alcoholic to hit bottom. But hitting bottom comes with a big price tag. The destruction of the family is one price many people pay. Hitting bottom can also mean jail, insanity, or death. Intervention is a way of *raising the bottom*. Intervening with *love first* helps an addicted loved one find recovery without going through years of affliction and loss. The family, too, is saved from heartbreak and pain that can endure for decades.

The fact that you have this book in your hands means you are probably ready to make a commitment for positive change. Roll up your sleeves and learn what needs to be done. You will be amazed at how things come together. As Napoleon Hill, researcher and writer on the philosophy of American achievement, discovered while observing successful people, "The moment you commit and quit holding back, all sorts of unforeseen incidents, meetings, and material assistance will rise up to help you. The simple act of commitment is a powerful magnet for help."

So trust the process, and take one step at a time. If, along the way, someone says, "You can't help an alcoholic until he's ready to accept help," politely ask what they think it'll take to get the alcoholic ready to accept help.

A Word about Terms We Use

Addiction is the same disease regardless of the drug used. Our society commonly differentiates mood-altering drugs by placing them in three major categories: alcohol, prescription drugs, and illegal drugs. Inhalants can be added to this list, but are substances not usually categorized as drugs. They are ordinary household solvents and substances that produce a high when sniffed. We describe addiction to these various drugs in different ways: alcoholism, drug addiction, and chemical dependency. All three words describe the same disease and are interchangeable. The recovery process is the same regardless of the drug of choice. While illegal drugs get the most attention from the media, alcoholism is the number one drug problem in the United States.

As you read this book, you will notice that we freely interchange the words alcoholic, addict, and chemically dependent. When we use the term *alcoholic,* we are talking about all addicted people regardless of their drug of choice. When we use the terms *addict* or *chemically dependent,* we are referring to people addicted to alcohol in addition to other drugs. Inhalants also are included when we use these terms.

Chemical dependency is an equal opportunity disease. It does not discriminate on the basis of race, age, education, economics, or sex. Keep in mind that addiction happens to both men and women, and to convey this, we have alternated the use of the pronouns *he* and *she.*

Are You Barking Up the Wrong Tree?

Just about everybody we talk to tells us they've tried everything to help the alcoholic and nothing works. But let's ask ourselves, what do they really mean when they say they've tried everything? Probably, *everything* means things such as reasoning, pleading, begging, rescuing, arguing, threatening, cajoling, bribing, ignoring, reprimanding, or punishing. Many of us have spent tremendous energy without making an inch of progress, because these efforts don't work—at least not for long.

So what's the problem? First of all, no one teaches us the right way to help someone suffering from alcoholism or other drug addictions. Turn on your television, pick up a newspaper. You'll see stories about drunken drivers, drug arrests, kids shooting heroin; but you'll rarely, if ever, see accurate, worthwhile information that prepares you to help your relative or friend. We ask our children to "just say no," but we don't teach them what to do if they marry an alcoholic or if their best friend becomes an addict. As a society, we focus on the problems of addiction but ignore solutions for the family. We have to change that, because chemically dependent folks aren't from another planet but from our families, our neighborhoods, our world. They are our friends and relatives. With the right information, we can make a huge difference.

Not long ago, we were at a grant-writing workshop in Lansing, Michigan. The instructor looked around the room and said, "You people who are working with alcoholics and addicts will have a tough time getting grants because people have no sympathy for alcoholics." He went on to explain that if we wanted financial support for our work, we needed to put a twist on what we do, such as helping children of alcoholics, preventing kids from using drugs, stopping drunken driving. Say anything, but don't say you want to help alcoholics. This illustrates the prevalent attitude we see throughout our country. We turn our backs on alcoholics and addicts and, when we do so, we turn our backs on the people who love them.

Is it any wonder that families are left empty-handed when it comes to coping with this disease? Renowned individuals step forward to educate us about breast cancer, AIDS, heart disease, diabetes, and Alzheimer's disease. On television commercials, a former presidential candidate is educating us about erectile dysfunction. But stop and listen for a word or two of sensible advice on how families can help an alcoholic, and you'll hear very little. You're left to your own devices, dreaming up ways to solve this problem on your own, randomly pulling ideas out of thin air. If one thing doesn't work, you try another. When that doesn't work, you come up with something else. You hope and pray the next thing works, but you end up frustrated again and again. It's no wonder you've come to the conclusion that nothing can be done. You're trapped in a catch-22: No one is teaching you the right approach, yet no one can expect you to know the right approach unless someone teaches it to you.

When You and the Alcoholic Are Speaking Different Languages

How many hours have you spent talking to your cherished loved one, trying to prevent him from sliding further into the quagmire of addiction? How did it feel when you saw that your best efforts were backfiring? Did a good intention look more like World War III? Alcoholics undoubtedly come out ahead, and you walk away scratching your head, trying to figure out what went wrong. Talking sense to an alcoholic is one of the most frustrating things you will ever do.

You probably don't realize that you and the alcoholic are speaking two different languages. To you, alcohol is the obvious problem and sobriety is the logical solution. If the alcoholic would listen, you know he would put the bottle down forever. Of course, it rarely works that way. To the alcoholic, alcohol is not the problem, it's the solution. The problem is anybody or anything that gets in the way of his consumption of alcohol. You're talking about alcohol as the problem; he's talking about you as the problem. See the problem?

To illustrate this point, consider Jeff's story. At twenty-six years old, Jeff was already in the latest stage of alcoholism. He couldn't hold down a job, eat solid food, or go more than four hours without a drink. He was living in a San Francisco city park when he couldn't panhandle enough money for a room in a flop house. He was bleeding internally and couldn't walk more than a short distance because of a nerve disorder caused by the toxic effects of alcohol. In the face of all this evidence, Jeff still didn't think he had an alcohol problem; he thought he had a cash flow problem. He wasn't thinking about recovery; he was thinking about suicide. Although his family tried many times to convince him to stop drinking, he didn't have the foggiest idea what they were so worked up about. He argued and saw them as the problem. Subsequently, he moved as far away from his family as he could. Jeff, another faceless alcoholic, almost died in the streets. It was only after his family learned how to speak to him differently that Jeff had a moment of clarity and accepted help.

As Dr. Vernon Johnson, the father of intervention, explains in his book *I'll Quit Tomorrow,* "The reason alcoholics are unable to perceive what is happening to them is understandable. . . . For many reasons, they are progressively unable to keep track of their own behavior and begin to lose contact with their emotions. . . . Alcoholics don't know what is happening inside of them."

The solution for addiction cannot come from a mind controlled by alcohol or other drugs. It must come from an outside source. Because we are the people who clearly see the problem, it is our job to bring a moment of enlightenment to the alcoholic. But first, we need to learn a language the alcoholic will understand.

When Keeping You Off Balance Is a Good Thing for an Alcoholic or Addict

How many times have you approached an alcoholic with your concerns, only to be blamed for everything? Suddenly, you're defending yourself, and the drinking problem gets lost in the shuffle. Every family we've talked with can relate to this blame game. Alcoholics and addicts use the blame game to deflect unwanted attention. It's a very effective technique. While you are busy defending yourself, the alcoholic is making his getaway. Keeping you off balance is a good thing for an alcoholic.

The alcoholic will do anything to keep you off his back. *Promise them anything* is one of his defenses. Alcoholics are very adept at convincing people they can handle the problem on their own, and you've probably been through this many times by now. The addict tells you that he'll change, and you hope with all your heart that this time he keeps his promise. However, because of his addiction, he's lost his ability to consistently keep promises.

"I'll stop using the hard stuff," the alcoholic may promise. She promises to drink wine instead of hard liquor, or the addict says she'll drink beer rather than smoke pot. She's switching to something that is perceived as less harmful, therefore, less problematic. There's a catch, of course. Switching to wine doesn't work, because alcohol is alcohol regardless of how it is delivered into the body. The formula for alcohol content is: One ounce of 86 proof liquor = twelve ounces of beer = four ounces of wine.

Each delivers the same amount of alcohol, so switching from one to the other is nothing but a shell game.

If the drug of choice is marijuana, cocaine, or some other illegal drug, the addict may appease you by promising to drink alcohol instead. Again, everybody is relieved because their treasured loved one is finally off "drugs." However, it's all chemistry to the brain. The brain doesn't say, "Oh, this is alcohol, a legal drug. Since we're not doing street drugs, we're not addicted anymore." When you switch one drug for another, it's called *switched addiction*. An addicted person cannot use any mood-altering drugs, including alcohol, without running into problems.

Another popular promise the alcoholic makes is, "I'll cut back." Most alcoholics, unless they're in the later stages of addiction, are capable of cutting back for periods of time. In the early and middle stages of addiction, the alcoholic doesn't lose complete control over his alcohol or other drug use. Instead he has periodic loss of control. For example, an alcoholic may cut back to two beers a day for a month. Then, one day, he can't stop at two beers and loses control. He contends that the month of responsible drinking proves he has control over his drinking when he sets his mind to it. However, as long as alcohol is entering his body, he will eventually have problems with the drug. Cutting back is never more than an unreliable, temporary fix for the alcoholic.

When an alcoholic finds herself in big trouble, she may take extreme measures to reconcile with you. She may promise: "I can prove I'm not an alcoholic. I'm going on the wagon." For the same reasons discussed above, chemically dependent people can be very successful at going on the wagon for varying lengths of time. Let us tell you the story of a man we worked with recently.

Bill began by telling us about the many wonderful years he and his wife have had together. However, near retirement, his wife's alcoholism had progressed to the point of destroying their relationship. He convinced her to visit a marriage counselor who rightly said that the relationship problems couldn't be dealt with as long as alcohol was still in the picture. The wife vigorously denied having an alcohol problem. The marriage counselor suggested something to the wife that made perfect sense to the untrained ear, but nonetheless was misguided and ill-advised: "If you're not an alcoholic, prove it to us by not taking a single drink for an entire year." With that, the wife left the counselor's office and obliged him by not drinking for one year. On the one-year anniversary, she opened up a bottle of wine and drank until she was inebriated. She proceeded to get drunk every day thereafter.

What happened here? First of all, the counselor didn't understand the concept of periodic loss of control—that only late-stage alcoholics have total loss of control over their drinking. His suggestion to go on the wagon implied that if the wife successfully stopped drinking for a twelve-month period, she wasn't an alcoholic. Contrarily, an alcohol and drug counselor would tell you that going on the wagon is a symptom of a drinking problem. It's called an attempt to control. Nonaddicted people don't strive to control their drinking, because they haven't lost control in the first place.

The wife, desperate to prove she wasn't addicted to drink, sacrificed alcohol for one year. Once the year was up, she felt she had her retribution and a well-deserved freedom from future accusations. Then she did what she'd been waiting to do all year—opened a bottle of wine, started drinking, and never looked back.

The husband, Bill, is once again living with an intoxicated wife, who reminds him that she had stopped drinking for the required amount of time and had proved she wasn't an alcoholic. The husband is left in a worse position than before he sought help. In this case, doing something was worse than doing nothing. The professional he consulted was a marriage counselor who didn't have sufficient knowledge about treating chemical dependency.

Be aware of why the alcoholic makes promises. The nature of addiction forces alcoholics and addicts to engineer escape routes whenever they feel threatened. Many of their promises are escapes. Remember, the alcoholic is protecting access to his solution—alcohol or other mood-altering drugs—while keeping you, "his problem," at bay. The more educated you become, the less likely it is you'll be persuaded by the alcoholic's diversions.

What Science Has Learned about the Genetics of Addiction

We often hear people blame their loved one's alcoholism on low self-esteem, stressful lifestyles, or marital problems. While all these may be reasons why people drink, they aren't reasons why people become alcoholic. If we look at people's drinking patterns, we'll probably see that they drink for different reasons at different times: beer is part of the fun with friends on weekends; scotch relieves stress after work; wine reduces inhibitions during a romantic date; martinis feel sophisticated at a fancy party. Which of these reasons—having fun, relieving stress, reducing inhibitions, feeling sophisticated—causes alcoholism? None of them, of course. Reasons for drinking can't cause addiction. If they could, everyone who drank for those reasons would be at high risk for alcoholism.

The majority of behavioral scientists and geneticists studying alcoholism agree that it's a genetic disease passed down from generation to generation. In 1990 researchers announced they found the gene that causes severe forms of alcoholism. The resulting media blitz led to wide public acceptance that the "alcoholic gene" had been discovered. Since that time, however, genetic researchers have announced that the study was not properly designed. Using correctly designed studies, geneticists find no evidence that this gene is responsible for alcoholism. Alcoholism and other addictions are more likely attributed to multiple genes rather than any one gene.

Dr. Robert Karp, program director for genetics in the National Institute on Alcohol Abuse and Alcoholism's Division of Basic Research, explains that alcoholism is one of the most complex diseases we know and a great challenge for scientists. Although researchers are making progress, Dr. Karp says that science must develop new scientific methods to meet the demands of studying the disease.

Dr. Karp goes on to say that even though researchers have not located the genes responsible for alcoholism, there is an overwhelming amount of evidence that alcoholism is inherited. This evidence has been gleaned through decades of adoption and twin studies that ask the question: "Does alcoholism run in families because children *learn* to become alcoholic; do they *inherit* genes that cause alcoholism; or *both*?" These studies consistently come to the same conclusion: alcoholism is an inherited disease, not a learned behavior.

Twin Studies

Twin studies separate genetics from environment by focusing on the differences between identical and fraternal twins: identical twins have the identical genes and fraternal twins have some of the same genes. If alcoholism is genetic, then identical twins should be equally predisposed to alcoholism because they have identical genes. In other words, if one identical twin is alcoholic, then the other is likely to be alcoholic; if one is nonalcoholic, then the other is likely to be nonalcoholic. Fraternal twin pairs should exhibit more differences in their predispositions to alcoholism because each twin has a different genetic makeup. In other words, more fraternal twin pairs will have one alcoholic twin and one nonalcoholic twin than will identical twin pairs.

If the influence is environmental, however, the probability that a pair of twins will match each other's predisposition to alcoholism will not change based on whether they are identical or fraternal twins. The probability of a match will be determined solely by the similarity of environments, not by the similarity of genes. So identical and fraternal twin pairs should show equal rates of matching each others' predispositions to alcoholism if each pair lives in the same environment.

After studying twins for decades, researchers find that differences exist between identical and fraternal twins. Identical twin pairs are much more likely to match each other in their predisposition for alcoholism than fraternal twins. Pairs of fraternal twins are more likely to differ in their tendency to be alcoholic, one twin being alcoholic while the other is not. This indicates that genes, not environment, determine alcoholism. It's inherited, not learned.

Researchers have also used twin studies to determine if addiction to other mood-altering drugs is genetic. The outcomes show that vulnerability for abusing marijuana, sedatives, heroin and other opiates, and hallucinogens is highly heritable. Some studies show different susceptibilities for different drugs. Dr. Ming Tsung, a researcher at Harvard, reports that "the genetic influence for abuse was greater for heroin than for any other drug." Researchers also find that abusing one type of drug is related to an increased vulnerability to every other type of addictive drug.

Adoption Studies

Adoption studies are another way researchers have separated genetics from environmental influences when studying alcoholism. Since the 1920s, researchers have studied people born of alcoholic parents but adopted at infancy into nonalcoholic homes. These studies may be the most effective at separating nature from nurture, genetics from environment. If environmental factors are responsible for alcoholism, adoptees born of alcoholic parents who grew up in nonalcoholic homes should show low rates of alcoholism. If genetics are responsible, adoptees will have higher rates of alcoholism regardless of their nonalcoholic upbringing. Researchers have found that adoptees born of alcoholics but raised by nonalcoholic parents are four times more likely to become alcoholic than adoptees whose biological and adoptive parents are nonalcoholic.

Animal Studies

Animal studies are also used to research the genetics of alcoholism. Scientists have genetically altered rats to develop strains of *alcohol-preferring* rats from rats who normally avoid alcohol. Alcohol-preferring rats will choose alcohol over water. Alcohol-avoiding rats will not drink alcohol even when deprived of water. When alcohol-preferring rats are bred, their offspring prefer alcohol too. When alcohol-avoiding rats are bred, their offspring avoid alcohol. This indicates that a low or high preference for alcohol is heritable. The American Psychological Association reports in the *APA Monitor* that "other trait models [using rats and mice] developed by researchers include . . . strains that sleep for a long time after drinking; strains that sleep a short time after drinking; strains that develop severe alcohol withdrawal symptoms after chronic alcohol exposure; and strains that develop mild withdrawal symptoms." Behavioral scientists say that the ability to breed animals to exhibit specific traits proves that these traits are genetically influenced.

Research consistently finds that the modeling of parental behavior does not account for the transmission of alcoholism. Children do not become alcoholic by watching the behavior of an alcoholic parent; they become alcoholic because they are genetically predisposed to the disease. But genetics alone don't account for alcoholism. A person must drink alcohol to activate the disease. For this reason, the National Institute on Alcohol Abuse and Alcoholism has issued statements recommending that people in alcoholic families abstain from alcohol use. Of course if family members don't know alcoholism runs in their family, they can't make an informed decision about whether or not to use alcohol. For this reason, hiding information about family alcoholism from children puts them at greater risk for becoming alcoholic. Be open with children. Tell them that alcoholism runs in your family and that they may have inherited the disease. Let them know that the only reliable way to prevent alcoholism is to choose not to drink. Moreover, be sure your words and actions are congruent. If you say "don't drink" but your actions say "drinking is terrific," your kids will probably follow your actions, not your words.

Animal, twin, and adoption studies consistently establish addiction as a genetic disease. Understanding addiction as a disease is not a new idea, however. In 1877 *Scientific American* published an article titled "Inebriety As a Disease." The article states: "Science . . . draws a broad distinction between drunkenness as a vice and drunkenness as a disease. The man who drinks for pleasure, it holds, may look for benefit in the counsels of others or in his own strength of will; but he who drinks because he cannot help it, being led by an irresistible impulse, is a sick man, and needs not a temperance pledge but a physician."

Eleven Misconceptions about Chemical Dependency

There is so much misinformation circulating about addiction, but not enough space here to discuss each myth in detail. Instead, we've selected the eleven most common myths. For each one, we'll give a synopsis of why it is not true. See how many of these you've accepted as fact:

1. *An alcoholic or addict must be ready for help before he can be helped.* We've already addressed this myth in the first section. A recent Hazelden survey of recovering addicts found that 70 percent found help after a friend, family member, employer, or co-worker intervened.

2. *You're not alcoholic if you don't drink daily or in the morning.* Patterns of alcohol or drug use can vary widely from person to person. While one alcoholic may drink every day, another may drink only on weekends or binge drink once every few months. It is not when or how much someone drinks, but what happens when they drink that will inform us if they have an addiction.

3. *You're not alcoholic if you still have a good job and never miss a day of work.* When someone has a problem with addiction, they're out to prove to themselves and to others that they are not addicted. Since one of the commonly accepted signs of addiction is absenteeism from the job, alcoholics often diligently go to work every day. Most addicted people are employed and many never miss work.

4. *Illegal drugs are more dangerous to the human body than alcohol.* Although illegal drugs are not safe, alcohol is the most dangerous drug to the human body. It affects virtually every organ of the body. Although there are studies as to the health benefits of alcohol, those benefits exist when alcohol is used in very small amounts and only for certain populations. For many people, the risks outweigh the benefits. Some studies counter the well-publicized findings as to how significant these benefits really are.

5. *Illegal drugs are the biggest addiction problem in our country.* Addiction to alcoholism far outweighs the problems associated with addiction to illegal drugs. Death from alcohol problems claims 100,000 people per year while drug-related deaths are approximately one-fifth that amount. Alcohol abuse costs businesses eighty billion dollars per year as compared to sixty billion dollars for all other drugs. Approximately eighty-seven million people are related to or living with an alcoholic, whereas about fifteen million are related to or living with a drug addict.

6. *Addiction is the result of a lack of willpower.* Chemical dependency is a complex disease that affects a person physically, mentally, emotionally, and spiritually. Willpower is not an effective therapy for this disease any more than it would be for cancer, diabetes, and heart disease. Addiction happens at a physical and psychological place that is beyond the reach of the will.

7. *A recovering cocaine (heroin, marijuana, speed, Valium) addict can still drink alcohol.* Alcohol is a mood-altering drug; therefore, no chemically dependent person can use alcohol and be in recovery from addiction. If a cocaine addict, for example, uses alcohol, it may set off cravings that will lead him back to cocaine use. If his use of alcohol continues, he will begin to show alcohol problems. This is called a switched addiction.

8. *An alcoholic can use Valium if he follows the doctor's directions.* A chemically dependent person should never use any addictive, mood-altering drugs even when prescribed by a doctor, except when absolutely necessary. Use of Valium or other mood-altering drugs on a regular basis activates addiction. Alcoholics may need a mood-altering drug if, for instance, they are in acute pain or going into surgery, but nonaddictive drugs or drug-free techniques are recommended for long-term medical needs. (Note that mood-elevating drugs or anti-anxiety drugs are not the same as addictive drugs.)

9. *If drugs are prescribed by a doctor there is no danger of becoming addicted.* While prescription mood-altering drugs have an important role to play in medicine, some people using these drugs become addicted to them.

10. *Addiction is the addict's problem, not mine.* Addiction is a family disease. Every chemically dependent person directly affects, on average, five to eight other people. Beyond the emotional and financial price paid by families and friends, addiction costs society billions of dollars.

11. *Treatment doesn't work.* For every dollar spent on treatment, we save society four to seven dollars. Treatment dollars are more effective at getting results than interdiction dollars (patrolling the borders for drugs) or law enforcement dollars. To get the same results as we get from treatment, the dollar amounts work out like this: It takes 246 million dollars in law enforcement or 366 million dollars in interdiction to get the equivalent results of 34 million dollars in treatment.

Myths and misconceptions originate from many sources. Please make a mental note that many health care providers, doctors, social workers, therapists, and psychiatrists are not trained in the field of chemical dependency. We recently read an article in one of the most respected newspapers in the country that was filled with erroneous information about addiction. A social worker told a friend of ours that her brother wouldn't need heroin if he lost weight and found a job he enjoyed. A book by a diet guru promises to cure alcoholism through nutrition. A doctor we know refers to alcoholism as a lifestyle choice. Don't grasp too quickly at the opinions presented by people who do not have proper training in the field of addiction.

SECTION

2

Understanding Family Responses

Good Intentions Can Take You down the Wrong Road

We hear the word *enabling* bandied about quite a bit, but what does it really mean to us? Is it possible that we could be contributing to the problem, even when we believe we're doing everything in our power to stop the addiction?

Almost all families inadvertently enable addicted loved ones by helping them avoid the negative consequences of addiction. For alcoholics and addicts to stay comfortable in their addiction, they need the help of the very people who want them to stop drinking. Family, friends, and co-workers are uninformed recruits, who unknowingly enable the addiction. Every alcoholic and addict has an enabling network or collection of people, professionals, or institutions whose combined efforts unwittingly allow addiction to continue flourishing in the addict's life. This happens in a number of ways, including loaning money, taking over responsibilities, making up alibis, covering up the problem, and allowing the alcoholic to manipulate them.

We must be vigilant against blaming each other for past enabling. Without proper guidance, we really can't expect otherwise from our families. People whose lives are touched by an alcoholic are trying to do the best they can with the information they have.

The other day, a friend of ours sent us a story titled "The Butterfly." The author is unknown, but it illustrates perfectly what we mean when we talk about enabling. The story begins with a man who came across a butterfly's cocoon. Fascinated, he stopped to watch as the butterfly struggled to free itself. After several hours, it appeared that the butterfly was stuck and unable to continue. Distressed by what he saw, the man decided to help. He took a pair of scissors and snipped away at the cocoon, and the butterfly emerged effortlessly.

But the butterfly's body was swollen and small, its wings were shriveled. The man waited, expecting the wings to enlarge and expand, the body to contract, and the butterfly to lift into the air. This did not happen. Unknown to the man, his act of kindness had interrupted the butterfly's natural struggle which forces the fluids from the body into the wings, preparing the butterfly for flight. The man's good intentions crippled the butterfly.

The story ends with this reflection: "Sometimes struggles are exactly what we need in our life. If God allowed us to go through life without any obstacles, it would cripple us. We would not be as strong as we could have been."

Like the butterfly, the alcoholic must be allowed to face his necessary struggles. When we help the alcoholic in ways that protect him from the natural consequences of his addiction, we may rob him of an opportunity to find his wings. We often hear recovering alcoholics and addicts warn, "Don't cheat an alcoholic out of his pain. It's the best friend he's got."

Remember, when we enable, our intentions are always good. But as the old saying goes, the road to hell is paved with good intentions. Explore examples of enabling behavior in "Tools" in section 6. Place a check mark next to any examples you recognize in yourself. Chances are, you'll see at least a few ways your best intentions unwittingly enabled the alcoholic. Make a commitment to stop repeating these behaviors you've identified and give the alcoholic the dignity to face his own, essential struggle.

Combine Love with Denial
and You Have Innocent Enabling

When someone important to us is in trouble, we do what we can to come to her rescue. It's a normal reaction. The strength of families is often measured by their ability to rally in a time of crisis. When a loved one has more than his share of problems, we explain the breakdown in many ways: bad luck, immaturity, rebelliousness, lack of self-discipline, stress, youthful inexperience, or low self-esteem. We surely don't leap to the conclusion that addiction is the source of the problem.

And why not? Alcoholism is not a rare disease. It claims one out of ten people. That may seem startling, but stop to consider that this number doesn't even take into consideration addiction to street drugs, inhalants, or addictive prescription drugs. One out of every three Americans is living with or related to someone with an alcohol or other drug problem. Yet, it's the last thing we consider when we're trying to identify the source of a loved one's troubles.

Even if someone were to say, "You know, Kathy's drinking has been worrying me lately," we explain the drinking away with some plausible excuse. We refuse to explore the issue further or consider any likelihood of addiction. A strong denial courses through the family. Alcoholism is an unacceptable diagnosis even in the face of much evidence. In our minds, addiction only happens to those people who are somehow less in control of

their lives, less vigilant to such failings. To admit that this affliction has visited our own family would be too threatening.

Another form of denial is the illusion that you have control
over whether or not you'll become addicted to alcohol or other
drugs. Many a self-confessed heavy drinker has explained away
any potential problems with alcoholism by saying, "I'm not worried about getting into trouble with alcohol. I'm keeping a close
eye on my drinking." The false premise behind this statement is
that a drinker can spot the problem of addiction before it happens and somehow cut it off at the pass. Recently, during a telephone conversation with a friend, we heard an example of this
form of denial. Our friend recounted a talk she had with her son.
She told him that there is a history of alcoholism on both sides
of the family, so he should be careful about his drinking. She
went on to explain that, although she and his dad drink, he
needn't worry because they were watching their drinking. The
truth of the matter is all people who begin using alcohol or
other drugs do so believing they are in control of their chemical
use. However, this belief does not change the fact that 10 to 20
percent of people who use mood-altering substances become
addicted and never foresee it happening. No one who drinks
chooses to be alcoholic, and no one chooses not to be.

The combination of this denial and our love for the addicted
person generates a type of enabling we call *innocent enabling*. We
help the alcoholic out of scrapes and messes, but we do not
know that alcoholism is the issue, and we don't even have a rudi-
mentary understanding that our helpfulness acts like fertilizer
to a growing addiction.

The first time Robert, a young man we knew, got in serious
trouble as a result of his alcoholism, nobody identified alcohol
as the problem. His parents' reaction is a perfect example of innocent enabling.

Robert was home from college for the holidays. His mother lent
him her beautiful new car for an evening out with his old high

school buddies. But Robert secretly had other plans. He stole away to a seedy old house where he could drink and find drugs. Once there, he spent hours smoking marijuana and drank six bottles of wine. By the time he left, it was three o'clock in the morning. Intoxicated and paranoid, he drove his mother's car toward home. When he saw a police car about a half-mile behind him, he kept his eyes locked on the rearview mirror, monitoring the cruiser's every move. He was so obsessed with the police car, he didn't see the car stopped at a red light directly ahead of him. Robert careened into the car at forty miles per hour without ever braking.

Although nobody was injured, Robert totaled both cars. The police pulled up, checked out the scene, and drove Robert home in the squad car. He was too drunk to speak coherently, so Robert's mom and dad just sent him to bed.

The next day, Robert's parents told him he'd have to pay for some of the costs related to the accident, but they never discussed how intoxicated he was the night before. Robert was their beloved son, the college student, the young man with a future. A son with a drinking problem wasn't part of the image they held close to their hearts. The idea that he was also using illegal drugs was even less imaginable.

The policemen thought they, too, were doing Robert a favor by not taking him to jail and ticketing him for drunken driving. The people he crashed into decided not to press charges. They knew Robert had been the president of the student association at the local high school and didn't want to cause him any embarrassment. Each person, in his own way, was an innocent enabler.

What if Robert's car accident had been caused by a seizure rather than drunkenness? They would have settled only for the best of medical care. However, when someone is arrested for drunk driving, we don't call for an assessment or for treatment. If we call anybody, we call an attorney.

Innocent enabling takes on many different forms. Here are other examples:

- A mother decides she cannot stand by while her grown son's house goes into foreclosure. She explains her son's problems away as a string of bad luck and writes a check to save the day. It never occurs to her that crack cocaine is behind all that bad luck.
- A colleague takes on additional work to cover for a friend's absenteeism and poor performance. She knows her friend is having trouble at home and wants to help her. She has no idea that her friend's problems at home and work originate from alcoholism.
- A daughter is suspended from school for drinking. Her parents find a half pint of vodka under her bed. They comfort themselves with the rationalization that all kids experiment, and she'll outgrow it.

People often say to us, "If only I'd seen the problem earlier, I could have done something then and things wouldn't be so bad now." None of us can solve a problem that in our minds doesn't exist. As we are reminded in the Al-Anon meditation book *Courage to Change,* "If my only way to cope with a difficult situation was to deny it, I can look back with compassion to that person who saw no better option at the time. I can forgive myself and count my blessings for having come so far since then."

Combine Reality with Fear and You Have Desperate Enabling

You round a corner and suddenly come face-to-face with reality. Denial is splayed wide open, and you can no longer refute the truth. It is addiction after all. What do you do next? Do you rush to find the best information on addiction? Do you ask friends how they successfully helped someone in their lives? Check books out of the library? Make appointments with addiction specialists? If you're like most people, the answer is no. Instead, fear grips you and catapults you into the next stage: *desperate enabling.*

On average, families wait seven years before reaching out for help, and the profile of desperate enabling takes on many shapes during this time. Once we know our beloved is indeed addicted, we work overtime to make sure we do not end up ruined by this blight. Our family's well-being is at stake. We can't face seeing one of our own ruined financially, incarcerated, or dead as a result of alcohol or other drugs.

To give you a clear picture of desperate enabling, we're going to recount an extreme situation we came to know through our work with families. We received a phone call from a woman who was very concerned about her brother's drug addiction and the way it was destroying her parents. She asked if she could bring her folks in to talk with us, and we met the next day. After an hour of talking, we learned some interesting things about this family.

The thirty-eight-year-old son we'll call Joe was addicted to crack cocaine and living at home with his retired parents. He moved in after losing his job and being evicted from his apartment. Mom and Dad realized drugs were behind his problems, but their son told them he wasn't ready to get help. So they naturally sought to protect him from any truly horrid consequences of his using. By keeping a close eye on him, they reasoned, they could at least keep him safe.

After three or four months, drug dealers began showing up at their door demanding payment for Joe's debts. He was buying crack cocaine on credit, and the drug dealers threatened to kill Joe if he didn't pay. The parents couldn't very well call the cops, because they'd have to confess that their son was on drugs. They said they certainly didn't want to get their son in trouble. So they paid off the huge sums of money he owed. Living on a fixed income, Joe's parents knew they couldn't continue paying off large drug debts, so they devised a plan. They told Joe they would give him a weekly allowance for crack cocaine and enough gas money to drive back and forth to the city where he bought drugs. In return, Joe agreed not to exceed his allotted budget for his drug purchases.

Over the next couple of months, Joe's parents felt they were successfully managing Joe's drug habit. However, on his trips to the city, he would be gone for three days, and return home looking like death. While away, he didn't sleep or eat, and his personal hygiene deteriorated. He visited a crack house and smoked crack around the clock. He came home only after he was so sick and broke he couldn't go on.

They welcomed him in, bathed him, fed him, and put him to bed. When he got his strength back and felt better, his cravings for crack would kick in. His parents would give him more money, starting the cycle again.

Pretty soon, the allowance wasn't enough. Things started disappearing from the house. One day he came home without his car. He said it had been stolen. In truth, he traded it to his crack dealer for more crack cocaine. So they began lending him their extra car. He gave that car away, too.

Joe's father decided he needed to come out of retirement and get a job. Joe's sister told us the family home was going up for sale because her parents were terrified of drug dealers showing up and killing everyone. Joe was still getting his crack allowance every week even though his parents were now several thousand dollars in debt. Joe's sister wanted to intervene on her brother and get him into treatment. We told her that intervention would likely succeed at motivating Joe to accept help if her parents would stop enabling Joe. This meant no more providing money. No more living at home unless he gets into recovery. Amazingly, Joe's parents did not feel they could follow through with that requirement. They held on to the illusion that they somehow had the power to save Joe from the consequences of his addiction. The reality of the magnitude of their son's problem, and their fear, kept them locked into desperate enabling.

You may be thinking that this is the most extreme story you've ever heard. It is extreme, but it isn't uncommon. Desperate enabling intensifies as the addiction intensifies. The more extreme the addiction, the more extreme the enabling. Ask yourself, "Am I doing things today that five years ago I would have said I'd never do?" As the addiction gets worse, we adjust and readjust to the problem. Our bottom line—the things we swear we'd never do—keeps receding out of a desperate need to save the addict from destroying himself.

Desperate enabling is born out of fear, and fear blocks us from moving out of this pattern. In their book *You Can't Afford the Luxury of a Negative Thought*, John-Roger and Peter McWilliams write,

> Most people approach a fearful situation as though the fear were some sort of wall. . . . But the wall of fear *is not*

real. It is an illusion we have been trained to treat as though it were real. . . . If fear is not a wall, what is it? It's a feeling, that's all. It will not [cannot] keep you from physically moving toward something unless you let it. It may act up and it may kick and scream and it may make your stomach feel like the butterfly cage at the zoo, but it cannot stop you. You stop you.

Our desperate enabling may lead us to unplanned and unimagined destinations. The alcoholic is more likely to stay in her addiction because she sees no compelling reason to change. As her chemical dependency progresses, she needs more and more of the drug to get the same results. Problems soar. Eventually she ends up in jail, goes insane, or dies as a result of her addiction. Loved ones who enable the alcoholic are at high risk for both physical and mental illnesses. Their stress may cause diseases in the family similar to those the alcoholic experiences.

According to Dr. Max Schneider, an internist specializing in families of alcoholics, the people around the alcoholic suffer from higher incidences of gastritis, stroke, heart disease, insomnia, respiratory problems, anxiety, and depression. Dr. Schneider warns that the risk of accidents, homicide, and suicide are much higher among families living with active addiction.

Desperate enabling causes every member of the family to suffer. Anger and disputes arise; blame is bounced from person to person; and the family unit itself is eventually damaged. Children are especially vulnerable to this phase of enabling. The adults in the family are so focused on keeping the alcoholic in line, they don't always notice what the children are going through. Make children your number-one responsibility. Be sure they are safe. Talk to them about alcoholism. Explain that it is a disease. It is nobody's fault, and the sick person can't help him- or herself. Give children a safe harbor, a person to talk to, and be honest with them. If you are aware of children who are living in danger because of a parent's addiction, it is your duty to act. For guidelines on helping children cope with a parent's alcoholism, contact the National Association for Children of Alcoholics. Their Web site is listed in the appendix.

In the third millennium, there is no reason anyone has to suffer silently as a loved one slips into chronic alcoholism. We have intervention; we have treatment for the alcoholic; and we have recovery for the family. Letting go of desperate enabling is the first step toward reaching these goals.

What Are the "Rewards" of Enabling?

Our instinct to avoid pain and seek pleasure is a fundamental source of motivation in our lives. Of these two drives, the desire to avoid pain is the most powerful.

Not long ago, we read a story about an eighty-year-old woman who runs marathons. She never ran a mile before she was in her sixties. We asked ourselves why someone would take up such a grueling sport at such an advanced age. Maybe she found great pleasure in setting and achieving difficult goals; but it was more probable, we thought, that marathons were a way for her to avoid the pain of aging by developing a superb physical condition required for the sport. Avoiding pain is the more powerful motivator.

The same holds true for the person controlled by alcohol or other mood-altering drugs. If she feels pain when not drinking or drugging, she'll drink to avoid the pain. If the pain of addiction becomes greater than the perceived pleasure of drinking, she's more likely to choose recovery. If family and friends interfere by easing the pain of addiction, they upset the ratio between pain and pleasure in favor of staying in the addiction. Said simply, we make drinking easier than not drinking.

Of course, the alcoholic is not alone in experiencing the pain of addiction. We, as family members, go through a gamut of difficult emotions. How do we escape our own emotional pain as our world seems to crash in around us? When addiction causes a problem, we are in pain, too; when the problem is solved, we're relieved and our pain is reduced. Our feelings of relief are a form of pleasure. Once we go through the enabling cycle a few times, we're conditioned to expect a reduction of pain and increased pleasure as a result of our enabling behaviors. Since we feel better, we mistakenly believe enabling works. Of course, since the addiction has not been treated, more problems will continue to surface. The only way we can keep up with the problems is to find more and more ways to enable. Our enabling progresses as the disease progresses, and our lives become increasingly unmanageable. Emotionally spent and exhausted, we start to feel like Alice in *Through the Looking-Glass* upon her first meeting with the Red Queen:

> "Now, Now!" cried the Queen. "Faster, Faster!" And they went so fast that at last they seemed to skim through the air, hardly touching the ground with their feet, 'til suddenly, just as Alice was getting quite exhausted, they stopped. . . . Alice looked around her in great surprise, "Why, I do believe we've been under this tree the whole time! Everything is just as it was! . . . In our country you'd generally get to somewhere else—if you ran very fast for a long time, as we've been doing."
>
> "A slow sort of country!" said the Queen. "Now, *here*, you see, it takes all the running *you* can do, to keep in the same place."

When addiction is the *country* you are living in, you'll be lucky if all the running (enabling) you can do keeps you in the same place. More likely, you end up in a worse place.

We spoke with parents of a twenty-seven-year-old woman suffering from alcoholism. They were particularly inventive at solving their daughter's problem of chronic unemployment. They decided to give their daughter her inheritance early, so she'd have a small income to keep her comfortably housed, clothed, and fed, regardless of whether she worked or not. The parents believed this plan would keep their daughter safe and, knowing she was safe, everything they did for their daughter felt right. The parents experienced a reduction in pain and an increase in pleasure as a result of rescuing their daughter from the problems caused by her alcoholism. Do you recognize the built-in reward system of their enabling behaviors? How will they most likely respond when this short-term solution topples over with the arrival of new problems?

Ask yourself a question: Knowing, as I do now, that an alcoholic must be allowed to experience the negative consequences of addiction, will I be able to allow that to happen *even when it is causing me pain?* Don't say yes too quickly. For most of us, if we are experiencing pain, our instinctual response is to ease that pain. If putting the alcoholic back on his feet is the only way we know how to reduce our pain, we will most likely enable the alcoholic. If we want to stop enabling the disease, we must first find a better way of managing our own pain, called *detachment.* Detachment means we stop managing the alcoholic's problems.

A story commonly heard in Al-Anon, a Twelve Step support group for families and friends of alcoholics, tells about a woman married to an alcoholic husband who fell out of bed whenever he was drunk, which was most nights. Each time he fell, the wife would get up and pull him back into bed. After attending a few Al-Anon meetings, she heard about detachment. The next time her husband tumbled off the bed, she left him to lie on the cold, hard floor all night. At her next Al-Anon meeting, she proudly told the story of her successful detachment. The other members said, "But, we meant to detach with love." The next time the woman's husband fell out of bed, armed with her new understanding of detaching with love, she wrapped a warm blanket around him as he slept the night on the floor.

Detachment helps us to choose to act rather than react, to begin letting go of problems that belong to someone else, and to do it all with love for the alcoholic. Detachment is the best solution to managing your pain in a way that frees you from enabling. However, detachment isn't easy. You'll do well to seek the support of a Twelve Step group for families and friends of alcoholics and addicts. Find an Al-Anon, Nar-Anon, or Families Anonymous meeting in your home area using the Resources in the Appendix or by looking in your local phone book.

Al-Anon's book *In All Our Affairs: Making Crisis Work for You* offers the following reflection: "Al-Anon helped me to focus my attention on what I could do about my situation instead of concentrating all my attention on what I thought the alcoholic should do. I was the one who had to take a stand."

Detachment: A New Recipe

The well-known "Serenity Prayer" by Reinhold Niebuhr is the perfect recipe for detachment: "God grant me the serenity to accept the things I cannot change, the courage to change the things I can, and the wisdom to know the difference."

We are encouraged to see what we cannot change in other people, places, and things, but what we can change in ourselves. What does it take to do this? *Wisdom and courage.* And what is the result? *Serenity.* When we detach with love, we take our focus off the alcoholic and place it onto ourselves. When we focus on ourselves, we regain our power to make meaningful choices about what we do and what we don't do. By making this shift in our thinking and actions, the world around us changes. Our world becomes manageable, and we find peace.

Many times people react vehemently against the idea that they should detach from the alcoholic's problems. They are sure their life will crumble if they don't continue holding up the alcoholic. However, focusing on the problem is one of the best ways to keep the problem alive. As long as our energy is spent managing the addiction, we are part of the problem. Detaching from the problem opens the door to solutions.

Successful CEOs and executives know this. The CEO of a Fortune 500 company told a reporter interviewing him that he never allows anyone to speak to him about problems. You might wonder how this man can run a huge organization if he won't let his people speak to him about problems. His response? "If someone comes in to tell me about a problem, I send them away. I tell them to come back when they can tell me about an opportunity or solution linked to that problem. Hearing about the problem doesn't do me any good—but an opportunity, now there's an altogether different matter. Then I know we're getting somewhere."

How do you turn an alcoholic's problem into an opportunity? Imagine you have a thirty-two-year-old son who works and lives in a nearby city. His own wife and kids moved out two months ago because of his drug problem. He's behind on his rent and has just received notice that in seven days they'll begin eviction proceedings. He's desperate. He calls you and says he has nowhere else to go. He'll lose his job if he's homeless. The entire scenario flashes through your mind and your knee-jerk reaction is to rescue him. Why not? He's your son.

Imagine stepping back from the problem. If you don't react to your son, but instead ask yourself, What choices do I have here?, you look for the opportunity and see it. Calmly, you explain to your son that you love him very much and want to help him. You've seen the effects drugs have had on his life. You ask him if he'd be willing to go into treatment as the solution to the problem. If he says yes, help him make immediate arrangements. Suggest he calls the employee assistance professional at his job to arrange admission into a drug rehab center that day. You explain that upon his admission to treatment you will help make payment arrangements with the apartment management. If he is in enough pain and has no other enablers to depend on, he'll very likely accept this offer of help.

If he refuses, you let go and stop trying to convince him further. You say, "It is your choice. If you change your mind, call me. I am willing to help, but only to help in the right way." By keeping your focus on yourself, rather than getting caught up in the crisis your son presented to you, you see an opportunity to act in a way that could lead to your son's recovery. But if your son refuses help, you can still feel good about doing the right thing.

You approached him with love, offered help, resisted enabling the disease, and left the door open for him to change his mind. Know that you are making choices that give him the best chance to choose recovery.

Napoleon Hill, the motivational writer who knew some of the greatest achievers in the history of our country, tells us, "It is virtually impossible not to become what you think about most. If you concentrate on something long enough, it becomes part of your psyche. . . . If you think about problems, you will find problems. If you think about solutions, you will find solutions. . . . The successful person understands this and learns to overcome them by focusing on the desirable objective, not on undesirable distractions."

If you are focused on the alcoholic, you are focused on the problem. Take your eyes off the problem, and you'll no longer be trapped in the problem. Put your focus on yourself. Resign from your job as manager of the alcoholic's problems. Sign up for the team that creates solutions.

As you continue to read this book, think about how the alcoholic's problems can give you some of the best ingredients for intervention. Memorize the "Serenity Prayer" so you know the recipe for detachment. Focus on you and how you can change what you do. Learn what you need to know in order to do this successfully.

Am I Seeing the Addict
as a Bad Person, or as a Sick Person?

As we delve into a discussion about addiction, pay close attention to what your head tells you versus what your heart tells you. It is not unusual to have an intellectual understanding of alcoholism as a disease, yet continue to react emotionally as if it were a moral failing or lack of personal discipline. Even professionals struggle with this, so don't beat yourself up over it. Just be aware of what is going on with you, so you can step back and see where your responses to the alcoholic are coming from.

Ask yourself these questions: At this moment, am I seeing the alcoholic as a bad person (a moral failing) or as a sick person (suffering from a disease)? How is my point of view coloring my reaction right now? If you're feeling angry and you want to yell at the alcoholic over a broken promise, back up and take a look at where this reaction is coming from. Can you readjust your thinking and readjust your expectations of him? Can you see that his disease blocks his ability to be reliable?

Addiction is a predictable, progressive, and chronic disease. The word *predictable* tells us there are certain symptoms we can reliably expect to see when alcoholism is present. We can organize those symptoms into a list and use that list as *diagnostic criteria*. The list is a tool that tells us what signs and symptoms indicate chemical dependency. The stage of addiction (early, middle, or late) is determined by the number of symptoms a person exhibits.

In the earliest stages of alcoholism, the symptoms may be so few that it is difficult even for a professional to make a reliable assessment. In the latest stages, the symptoms are so numerous just about anybody could make a diagnosis of addiction.

The term *progressive* means that without treatment the problem always gets worse. Unchecked, addiction eventually leads to incarceration, insanity, or death. Halting the progression requires abstinence. Long-term abstinence is most likely achieved when the alcoholic works a program of recovery in Alcoholics Anonymous or another Twelve Step program. The medical community may treat other physical and psychological illnesses that co-exist with the addiction, but the Twelve Steps are crucial to long-term, contented sobriety.

In Finland, a study of recovering alcoholics showed that the only significant predictor of length of sobriety at ten years after treatment was an ongoing participation in the fellowship of Alcoholics Anonymous. Of course, there always is a story about an alcoholic who put the bottle down without a recovery program and hasn't had a drink since. This happens. But an alcoholic without a program of recovery is at high risk of returning to alcohol use in days, months, or years. In addition, an alcoholic without recovery rarely finds the quality of life in her sobriety as compared to those in a Twelve Step program.

Even if the addict is abstaining from drug use, without recovery the symptoms of the disease may continue to progress. The alcohol is out of the picture, but the alcoholic behavior is not. Abstinence is only the first step. The ultimate goal of recovery is contentment, serenity, and joyous relationships. The Big Book, published by Alcoholics Anonymous, states:

> A.A. does not teach us how to handle our drinking. . . . It teaches us how to handle sobriety. . . . I guess I always knew the way to handle my drinking was to quit. . . . It's no great trick to stop drinking; the trick is to stay

stopped. . . . A.A. . . . led me gently . . . to embrace reality
with open arms. And I found it beautiful! For at last, I
was at peace with myself. And with others. And with
God.

During the downward progression of the disease, the alcoholic
will have moments of improvement. These moments can obscure
the forward march of the disease from the eyes of family and
friends. Look at the whole picture rather than specific points in
time to identify the increasing damages caused by addiction.

The word *chronic* reminds us that there is no cure for chemical
dependency. Once a person is addicted to alcohol or other
mood-altering drugs, there is no going back to drinking as a
nonalcoholic. The best we can do is put the disease in remission.
A medical diagnosis may read like this: "Alcoholism: arrested."
No amount of time without alcohol or other drugs can change
this diagnosis to: "Alcoholism: cured." There is no cure. A return
to drug use reactivates the disease. An old saying used among recovering people and addiction professionals is, "Once you're a
pickle, you can never be a cucumber again."

People often ask us how you can tell if a person is actually addicted to alcohol or other drugs. For a layperson worried about a
friend or relative, you can ask yourself one question: "Is the person experiencing repeated negative consequences in any area of
his life due to alcohol or other drugs, and does he continue to
drink anyway?" If you answer yes, the person you are concerned
about is probably chemically dependent and would benefit from
a professional assessment by an addictions counselor. If you are
interested in the specific symptoms and stages of alcoholism,
turn to the Jellinek chart (see page 244).

To learn everything you'd ever want to know about the disease of alcoholism, and actually have fun doing it, read the book
Loosening the Grip by Jean Kinney and Gwen Leaton. A quote from
the book underlies what we are striving to say: "Alcoholism—

alcohol dependence—has not always been distinguished from drunkenness. Alternatively, it has been seen as a lot of drunkenness and categorized as a sin or character defect. The work of E. M. Jellinek was largely responsible for the shift from a defect to an illness model. In essence, through his research and writings, he said, 'Hey, world, you folks mislabeled this thing. You put it in the sin bin, and it really belongs in the disease pile.' How we label something is very important. It provides clues how to feel and think, what to expect, and how to act." By understanding that addiction is a disease, not a choice, you will approach the problem differently.

Addiction is neither something the alcoholic does to us nor a moral failing. Many people of tremendous accomplishment succumb to this illness. Unimpeachable character is not a vaccine against chemical dependency—addiction is an equal opportunity disease. Yes, it's true that people have to choose to drink before they can become alcoholic, but we live in a society that promotes drinking. Mood-altering drugs are widely prescribed to help people sleep, calm down, cope with stress, and escape pain. Illegal drugs are readily available any place you go—even in maximum security prisons—and are considered fashionable in some social circles. When we use mood-altering drugs of any type, we can expect that a certain percentage will become addicted to those drugs, period. Once the choice to use a mood-altering drug is made, it is anybody's guess as to who will or will not become chemically dependent.

Using the Power of the Group

Believe it or not, intervention is more about us than about the alcoholic. Certainly, our motivation to intervene comes from the problem of addiction. And, yes, our goal is to deliver the alcoholic into treatment, followed by a program of recovery and a contented sobriety. But when all is said and done, intervention is about taking our eyes off the alcoholic and putting the focus on ourselves. It is about what *we* choose to do and not do. It is about choosing to reach out to the alcoholic with love and honesty, about acting in a way that preserves the alcoholic's dignity, and about moving into the solution and giving the alcoholic an opportunity to do the same.

To motivate an alcoholic to accept help requires a new outlook. The first thing to realize is that one-on-one confrontations with an alcoholic rarely work. Alcoholics and addicts are skillful manipulators and on your own you lose. Dealing with alcoholism effectively—whether in the family, in a treatment center, or in Alcoholics Anonymous—is all about working in groups. The power of the group can triumph over the power of addiction. One-on-one, an alcoholic can manipulate even a well-trained addictions counselor, but not a well-trained group. Groups are the driving force behind intervention.

In recovery circles you always will hear people refer to the *power of the group*. The first word of the Twelve Steps is *we*. It is common to talk in terms of the *we* of recovery.

The next section of this book will teach you how to work in a group, how to think in terms of *we*. Approaching the alcoholic one-on-one saps all your power. There are exceptions to this rule, but we'll leave that discussion for later, in section 4.

Do remember that intervention is a process, not an event. Intervention teaches you a new way of dealing with chemical dependency and asks you to use what you've learned from this time forward, not just during the half hour or so it takes to do an intervention. Make a commitment to the process of intervention, not just to a one-time event.

One of the first questions people ask us when talking about intervention is, "How successful is it?" Statistically, success ranges between 80 and 85 percent—if we define success as motivating the alcoholic to accept help. However, we believe all interventions, correctly done, are successful. Four primary reasons make every intervention a success: (1) the family is united through education and open communication; (2) the addicted person hears how much her family loves her; (3) the family has an opportunity to explain how the addiction has affected them; and (4) the addict learns that the family will support recovery but not addiction.

The single fact that the family has finally come together as a group, learned about the disease of chemical dependency, and perhaps for the first time talked about the problem and its solution makes intervention a success. Although individual family members may have known about the addiction for years, intervention is often the first organized attempt by the entire family to work toward a remedy.

The second reason for success is that during the intervention, the alcoholic hears, in very specific terms, how much she is loved. Most of us will live and die and never experience a time when the people we care about come together in one room, at one time, to tell us how much they love us and why. Take a moment to imagine that experience. Close your eyes. Picture a pleasant room with a circle of chairs. Think of the people closest to you sitting in those chairs. Now, go around the circle listening to each person reveal to you how much he or she loves you. Hear them describe the special qualities they cherish in you and the memories of you they hold dear to their hearts. Be still and notice how you feel as you visualize this experience. As you can imagine, this is an overwhelming emotional encounter for an alcoholic who feels anything but lovable.

Another reason for success is that the alcoholic finally hears how her addiction has affected those people who love her. There is no anger, there is no blame, only honesty and love. Even if the alcoholic refuses the help offered to her, these words from her family and friends will resonate in her mind for a long time. She can't forget them. This will profoundly affect her future drinking.

Finally, the alcoholic learns that the people closest to her no longer intend to enable the disease; but instead, each person has made a commitment to support only recovery. She is told she can turn to anyone in the group at any time. They will do whatever they can to help her get into recovery, but no one is now willing to help her stay sick. Accomplishing this much is a huge success. After laying down these ground rules, many a "failed" intervention turns itself around in a few days, weeks, or months, once the alcoholic reflects on her situation and decides to reach out for help after all.

Intervention is not a complicated process, but it does require planning and preparation. If you want the best results, follow the directions to the letter and don't cut corners. As Norman Vincent Peale tells us in *The Power of Positive Thinking*, "It is not enough to know what to do about difficulties. We must also know how to do that which should be done."

One last word before we move on to the next section. If an alcoholic's behavior is endangering a child, including an unborn child, or setting up dangerous situations such as drunken driving or domestic violence, the alcoholic relinquishes the right to choose. Although we cannot control an alcoholic's actions, we do need to control how we respond to those actions. Take the necessary steps to safeguard defenseless victims, even if that means calling the police.

Not too long ago, we were contacted by a man who learned his wife had taken their three-year-old son on a drug deal and then smoked crack cocaine in the car while the child was in the back seat. This man rightly went to court to request suspension of the mother's visitation rights. In another case, a woman called us to initiate an intervention after her husband drove drunk with their daughter and son in the car. She said, "I've put up with a lot due to his drinking, but I promised myself I'd draw the line if he ever put our children's lives in jeopardy." She successfully intervened on her husband's alcoholism, but if he hadn't accepted help, she was prepared to ask him to move out of the house as a way of protecting their children. Addiction increasingly diminishes the addict's ability to make responsible decisions. Take swift and appropriate action if poor decisions on the part of the addict are endangering others or himself.

SECTION

3

Preparing for an Intervention

Building a Team

Dante once wrote, "A mighty flame followeth a tiny spark." You are about to do a powerful thing. You are getting ready to pick up the phone to call the people closest to the alcoholic and ask them if they are willing to learn about something that could save the alcoholic's life. With every call you make, you ignite a spark.

Building a team gives you the best possible chance of defeating addiction. Your success depends on the help of a well-selected group of three to eight individuals working together. Intervention requires that a team of people who care about the alcoholic come together to work in the power of the *we*.

Selecting a team for an intervention starts with making a list of all the significant people in the alcoholic's life. These are the people the alcoholic loves, respects, depends on, needs, likes, and admires. You'll find names for your list among relatives, friends, co-workers, employers, clergy, teachers, and medical professionals. Turn to "Building a Team" in section 6 and use the worksheet to write down everyone who comes to mind. Don't edit anyone out just yet, and don't start calling anyone. Right now, you are creating a preliminary list from which you will select your final team. Only then will you begin making telephone calls.

As you fill out the list, begin with relatives. Then write down friends and finally other important people such as employer, co-workers, minister, doctor. Not all of these people will necessarily participate in the intervention, but we want their names on our list. We may use their help in other ways besides attending the intervention.

If people live far away, don't exclude them from your list. If you're thinking, "Oh, Jack can't make it. He lives eight hundred miles away and has a demanding work schedule and three kids." Let people decide for themselves. We've found that people go to great lengths to help a loved one. In one case we worked on, every family member and close friend of the alcoholic lived in a different state except for the parents. When the alcoholic's parents started calling, each sibling and friend they asked to participate said yes. Everybody took time off work, arranged for child care, and made airline reservations. When the alcoholic walked into his parents' house at the time of the intervention and took one look at all the people assembled in the living room, he knew why they were there. Before anyone said a word, he announced, "Okay, I'll go." The alcoholic, so strongly affected by seeing his friends and family from all over the country in one room, realized there was only one reason for them to be gathered together at his parents'—his alcoholism. Don't underestimate what people will do to help someone they love.

However, when you call people to discuss the possibility of intervention, you may get a mixed reaction. Some people may be very enthusiastic, others somewhat reluctant, and still others may be fiercely opposed. Meet everybody at their starting points. Before you pick up the phone, tell yourself you are giving permission for that person to express his or her feelings *even if they're different from your own.* Each person has had his or her own unique experiences with the alcoholic, and it's not uncommon for family members to feel angry or fed up. The idea of an intervention may not be welcomed with open arms. That's all right. Don't try to talk people out of how they feel. Let people have their feelings. Listen to them. Have empathy. Put your agenda aside long enough to hear what they have to say. They'll give you valuable information about the toll addiction has taken on them. How they feel gives you your starting point.

Set realistic goals for yourself before you begin building your team. Before you place a call, ask yourself, "What do I want to accomplish with this first conversation?" Business people often say that the only goal they have for their first meeting with a new client is getting the second meeting. Start by setting up realistic goals for yourself. For instance, consider asking relatives and friends to agree to learn about intervention. This is a comfortable first step for most people. Your first conversation might begin with something like this: "I see things getting much worse with Johnny, and I'm very worried about him. I've been learning about how we might help him in a way we've never tried before. It's called intervention, and it's done with a great deal of love and care. Would you be willing to learn a little bit more about intervention with me? Maybe we'll find it's something we want to do and maybe not. But I don't think we can lose by taking a look."

If the person you're asking launches into all the reasons why Johnny is beyond help, don't interrupt. Let her express her frustration. All of her previous experiences tell her that Johnny is a hopeless case. Once she's finished saying what she needs to say, you can respond with something like, "I know how frustrating this is, but I thought it wouldn't hurt to find out a little more. I love Johnny and I know you do, too. Would you be willing to join me just to look into it?" Even the person most fed up with Johnny is likely to agree to that much. She doesn't have to believe Johnny can be helped or that intervention works, she just has to agree to learn about it. That is a successful first step.

Approaching people about doing an intervention can be stressful and emotional. You don't know how people are going to react to the idea—or to you. Fearing a negative reaction can sometimes be enough to keep you from asking at all. First call the people you think will support you. Get them on the team first. Then call the relatives and friends who may be more reluctant. By naming other family members willing to learn about intervention, others may be more comfortable with saying yes, too.

This is an example of how the power of the group can be more effective than one individual.

If you are concerned about talking to someone who is a tough prospect, perhaps one or two family members who are supportive of intervention can talk to that person with you. Keep in mind that it's okay for someone to be reluctant. Reluctance is only a starting point. It tells you he needs more information. Don't expect him to meet you at the point where you are—respect his feelings. Remember, those feelings are coming from repeated experiences of hurt, frustration, and disappointment. You might say to him, "I don't blame you for feeling the way you do. In fact, with what you've been through with Johnny, I can't imagine you feeling differently than you do. What we're suggesting doesn't erase the past, but it might change the future for the whole family as well as for Johnny. Will you just come learn about it with us?"

If this person still doesn't want to participate, respect his wishes. Don't force the issue. Stay on good terms with him, letting him know that the door is always open.

As you build your team, one person's reluctance to participate shouldn't stop you in your tracks. Things have a way of falling into place if you keep moving forward. As comedian Gracie Allen once said, "Never place a period where God has placed a comma." Keep moving ahead, even if you feel like you've hit a brick wall. Brick walls often turn out to be nothing more than mist—you can't see past them, but if you keep walking, you get through them easily enough.

A Few Things to Consider
Before Picking Up the Phone

You may already know who will be on your intervention team, but there are a few considerations before you begin making phone calls. Be sure each person you plan to ask is appropriate for the intervention before you talk to them. Use the following guidelines to screen each person on your list.

Exclude anybody on your list who is actively chemically dependent. A practicing alcoholic or addict should not be on a team intervening on another addict or alcoholic. He may sabotage the intervention. He may turn against the team in the middle of the intervention, become angry and defensive, or minimize or rationalize the alcoholic's problems. This creates instability on the team—dangerous to any intervention.

Many times family members worry about their own drinking history with the alcoholic. They fear the alcoholic will say, "Hey, how can you say anything to me? I've seen you do your share of drinking." A history of social drinking with the alcoholic is not a problem and should not keep anyone from participating *as long as they are not chemically dependent themselves.* We'll discuss this issue in more detail later in the book. For now, cross any person with an active alcohol or drug problem off your list.

Next, is anybody on your list likely to tell the alcoholic about the intervention ahead of time? Some people think they're doing the alcoholic a favor by warning him about the intervention. If someone on your list is incapable of keeping it a secret, don't ask her to be on the team. If an alcoholic learns about the intervention, the intervention will fail. By notifying the alcoholic in advance, his natural reaction is to build up defenses that protect the disease and keep you out.

A few years ago, we facilitated an intervention that had all of the elements for success. The key people were all in attendance: the wife, mother, father, sisters, brother, a favorite uncle, the best friend, and the boss. We had a letter from the family doctor recommending treatment for alcoholism. Everything was beautifully planned, and everyone was highly prepared. The alcoholic showed up on time, sat down, and listened to everybody. The intervention went without a hitch—until we asked the alcoholic to accept help. Instead of agreeing, he unemotionally announced to the group that he did not need help, thanked everybody for expressing their opinions, stood up, and calmly walked out. We were stunned. We quickly learned the reason behind the calculated and cold response we got. His wife, in a fit of rage toward the alcoholic, told him about the intervention a week before it took place. He had seven days to think and plan. He hardened himself against his family and friends. All the love expressed during the intervention had zero effect on him. The intervention was doomed before it began. Don't tell anyone about the intervention who might tell the alcoholic. Explain to each person why the alcoholic can't be told.

The last thing to consider is whether anyone on your list is strongly disliked by the alcoholic. If so, they should not participate. We use love to reach the alcoholic. If the alcoholic feels disdain for a particular person, there's no love to work with. Obviously, many people in the family have had arguments or bad feelings with the alcoholic. There may be sibling rivalries. But the alcoholic still loves these people regardless of the problems. What we're concerned about is deep-seated resentment or conflict that goes way beyond disagreements or bickering. If the alcoholic has such a potent dislike for somebody, that person is not appropriate for the intervention team.

Sometimes there are extenuating circumstances and excluding someone from the intervention won't work well. We were contacted by the parents of a heroin addict to plan an intervention. The addict's sister had been so angry with him, she hadn't talked to him in two years. We didn't think intervention was the appropriate setting for a reunion between the two, but we did feel she should have a presence. Her brother needed to hear she was involved and she cared. It was decided that although she would not attend, she would write a letter to her brother. She asked her mother to read the letter for her during the intervention. She began the letter by writing, "Even though I stopped talking to you, I never stopped loving you. I just didn't know what else to do."

During the planning stages of another intervention, we were told that the alcoholic "hated" her brother-in-law. Our first response was to say that he couldn't participate, but things were more complicated than that. We learned that the alcoholic had never told her sister how much she disliked her husband. The consensus was that opening this can of worms before the intervention would cause a serious rift in the family, and the sister of the alcoholic might refuse to attend the intervention if her husband were excluded.

After discussing this problem thoroughly, we settled on a compromise. We included the brother-in-law in the intervention but placed him in a chair slightly out of the alcoholic's direct view. We minimized his negative impact by sandwiching his involvement between two people for whom the alcoholic had great respect and love. We diplomatically suggested he keep his letter to the alcoholic short, and we edited the letter for anything that could trigger anger. In the end, the strained relationship did not disrupt the intervention, and the alcoholic agreed to treatment. There are times when things are not black and white, and we need to make judgment calls. Take time to problem solve and you'll find workable solutions.

Involving Doctors and Other Professionals

Before you talk to a doctor about your plans for intervention, get your family and friends on board first. Work with your team while you decide how, and if, to contact the addicted person's doctor. Use the following guidelines to help you make your decisions.

A letter from a doctor recommending treatment can be a powerful tool during an intervention. It is particularly helpful if the addict is using prescription mood-altering drugs, since he may falsely believe he can't be addicted to a drug prescribed by a doctor. Since the addict probably has numerous doctors prescribing drugs to him—informally referred to as *shopping docs*—contact the addict's physician and let him know about the drug problem. Before you call the doctor, gather as much information as you can. Find out the types of drugs being used, how many doctors are prescribing, and the drug-related behaviors you've witnessed. The more information, the better.

When talking one-to-one, doctors may advise alcoholic patients to quit drinking, but alcoholics cannot quit so easily. The physician might say, "You have the beginnings of cirrhosis. This is a serious life-threatening condition, and if you continue drinking you'll die." The alcoholic, truly shaken by the news, tells the doctor he's had it with booze, and that he'll quit drinking immediately. But the next day he's drinking again. He truly meant to quit, but his disease of alcoholism is more powerful than his fear of death. A doctor talking to an alcoholic one-to-one usually doesn't get very far, but in the context of an intervention a doctor's recommendation can be powerful.

Alcohol is the most damaging drug to the human body. It affects all organs. In a report to the National Institute on Alcohol Abuse and Alcoholism at the National Institutes of Health, it was estimated that 30 percent of patients in hospitals have alcohol-related illnesses, and that alcoholism is as common as coronary disease among the elderly. Yet many doctors have difficulty diagnosing alcoholism. According to a 1992 study published in the *Journal of Studies on Alcohol,* doctors with special training in addictions failed to identify 65 to 84 percent of their patients with alcohol-related problems. Families are often frustrated when their loved one comes home with a glowing report of physical health from the family practitioner, but alcoholism was easily overlooked.

In some cases, doctors fear that questions about alcohol use will offend their patients, so they gloss over the issue or ignore it completely. Other times, an illness caused by the toxic effects of alcohol is treated but the alcoholism is not. For example, chronic alcoholism can cause certain heart problems. A doctor may prescribe heart medication for a patient with arrhythmia or other abnormalities without ever assessing the patient for alcoholism.

Sometimes a doctor's personal relationship with alcohol interferes with his ability to diagnose alcohol problems in others. Remember, one out of ten doctors is a daily drinker. Doctors using alcohol every day may not be as concerned about patients who are abusing alcohol. A doctor is apt to view drinking patterns similar to his own as normal. If the doctor is a heavy drinker, he may find the alcoholic's drinking less of a concern than does the family.

Every so often, we'll come across a doctor treating alcoholism with Valium or similar drugs. We recently worked with a sixty-five-year-old alcoholic woman whose doctor did just that. It didn't take the woman long before she was mixing Valium with large amounts of alcohol—a deadly combination. Valium is not a treatment for alcoholism; it's a switched addiction. A doctor making these kinds of recommendations may be a big hit with the alcoholic, but not to the family.

Many doctors are not knowledgeable in the area of chemical dependency. In four years of medical school, doctors may get as little as two hours of education on the number-one problem in America. If your attempt to work with a doctor fails, it may be that he or she is unprepared to deal with chemical dependency. A good bet is to look for a doctor who is an addictionist and a member of the American Society of Addiction Medicine (ASAM). These doctors have completed special education in the area of chemical dependency. For a referral to an ASAM-certified doctor, call 301-656-3920 and ask for the membership assistant, or send e-mail to **www.asam.org.**

Doctors who have a good understanding of chemical dependency are often very helpful and supportive of intervention. When asked, they gladly write letters recommending treatment. Someone selected from the team can read the doctor's letter during the intervention. Don't expect a doctor to attend an intervention unless he or she is also a close family friend.

If the family doctor isn't familiar with assessing chemical dependency, suggest he read "The Physicians' Guide to Helping Patients with Alcohol Problems," a pamphlet published by the National Institute on Alcohol Abuse and Alcoholism (NIAAA). The twelve-page pamphlet can be downloaded and printed off the Internet by logging on to **http://silk.nih.gov/silk/niaaa1/ publication/physicn.htm.** Or call 301-443-3860 and ask for publication number NIH Pub. No 95-3769. NIAAA will send you a copy at no charge.

You can use the same guidelines as you would for doctors when asking other professionals—such as a counselor, social worker, or psychologist—to write letters for the intervention. Keep in mind, some professionals do not understand that chemical dependency is a primary disease, and they may be prone to explain it away as a symptom of another problem. You must be vigilant in your expectation that the addiction be treated as a primary disease.

While writing this book, we learned that a relative of ours is addicted to prescription drugs. Her insurance company sent her to see a psychiatrist. Although she asked for treatment at a chemical dependency center, the psychiatrist instead directed her to a psychiatric hospital and diagnosed her with major depression. When our relative explained she wasn't depressed and had never experienced symptoms of major depression, the psychiatrist dismissed her objections. He said addiction was caused by depression. This is incorrect. Some people who are addicted are depressed, but depression doesn't cause chemical dependency. If you remember only one thing from this section, remember this: *Addiction is a primary disease, not a symptom of something else.* You might write this on a slip of paper and carry it with you. Other problems may coexist with the addiction—and often do— but the addiction must be dealt with before the other problems can be solved.

If a professional talks to you about addiction as a symptom of something else and wants to focus on that instead of the addiction, an alarm should go off in your head. If your house is burning down, you're not going to waste time talking to the firefighters about your bad plumbing. If the professional you're working with wants to talk about depression, or low self-esteem, or childhood issues while your loved one is in the throws of addiction, look for a more knowledgeable professional. Call someone at a local alcohol and drug treatment center for suggestions. He or she usually will know the doctors, psychiatrists, psychologists, and counselors who understand chemical dependency.

Involving the Workplace

In preparing an intervention, contacting the workplace causes family members more concern and fear than any other issue. They fear the addict will be fired once the boss learns of his alcohol or other drug problem. It is more likely, however, that the company has policies supporting treatment and recovery.

Ignoring the work issue only invites the alcoholic to use his job as an ironclad reason why he can't accept help. When you are in the middle of an intervention, the alcoholic may say, "I can't go to treatment because I'll lose my job." You want to be prepared to say, "We've followed company policy and made the necessary arrangements for your medical leave. Your job will be waiting for you when you are finished with the treatment program."

A family came to us after their thirty-two-year-old alcoholic son was hospitalized for esophageal varices, a rupture of the veins along the esophagus caused by chronic drinking. The rupture led to massive bleeding and their son nearly died. After a few days out of the hospital, he started drinking again. The family decided intervention was their last hope to save him. Before the intervention, we explained to the family that they must contact the workplace and arrange for a medical leave. In this particular case, the alcoholic's father was a long-time friend of the employer, and he agreed to make the phone call. We decided that if the alcoholic used work as an objection to treatment, the father could explain he had talked to the boss and made all necessary arrangements for a medical leave. As we predicted, the son used his job as an objection to treatment. We turned to the father, expecting him to speak, but found out he hadn't called the boss after all. We had no way to refute the alcoholic's objection. Seeing all was lost, the father reached for the phone and called the boss right there and then. He explained that the family was in the middle of doing an intervention on the son. The boss replied, "It's about time. Tell him he'll keep his job, but I don't want to see him back here until after he completes treatment." With that news, the son changed his mind and went to treatment immediately.

Calling the boss directly may not be appropriate for everyone. There are a few other ways you can approach the workplace. Many companies provide an employee assistance program, or EAP. Call the workplace for the telephone number of the EAP. You do not have to say who you are or why you want the number. When you talk to the EAP, ask if your conversation will be kept confidential. Once you know confidentiality will be maintained, explain that you are planning an intervention on a relative who is an employee, and you need to know the company's policies regarding medical leave for chemical dependency treatment. The EAP will give you guidelines to follow. By following the company's policies, you'll protect the alcoholic's employment status and strengthen your position during the intervention.

Some families worry that a company may support treatment and fire the alcoholic later. Addiction is a problem most companies face and firing recovering people is not common practice. Businesses invest huge sums of money to train employees— whether you're in the mail room or the boardroom. Employee turnover is costly. It's smarter to help employees solve problems than to fire them. Even if an employer did try to fire someone for addiction, the Americans with Disabilities Act prohibits discrimination against people seeking help for chemical dependency. An alcoholic is more likely to get fired if she doesn't seek treatment. No law will stop an employer from firing someone who is missing work or performing poorly due to alcohol or other drugs.

If you are dealing with a company or small business that does not have an EAP, contact a co-worker of the alcoholic. He or she can tell you about company policy or the best person to contact for information. Or you can call the human resources department anonymously and ask them about the procedures for taking a medical leave. Keep in mind that human resources personnel are not bound by confidentiality, so if you choose to identify the alcoholic by name they may pass the information on to management. Some families contact the boss directly if he or she is reputed to be fair and supportive.

If you decide you cannot contact the workplace under any circumstances, you will be at a disadvantage during the intervention. You can minimize the disadvantage by scheduling the intervention early in the weekend—Friday afternoon (only if he's sober) or Saturday morning. If the alcoholic says he can't go into treatment because of work, ask him to check in for a three-day assessment and detox on Saturday, Sunday, and Monday. Monday will count as a sick day, and the attending physician will write a doctor's excuse to give to the boss. Once detox is complete, the alcoholic can be transferred to an evening outpatient program so he can work during the day. This is appropriate for people who need a short medical detox and who don't need the extra support of an inpatient program. You should discuss this plan with the treatment center staff. A fall-back plan is better than no plan, but you'll always have a stronger hand if the workplace issues are resolved before the intervention.

One family we worked with called the boss about the intervention even though they didn't know how he would react. Knowing how sick their son was, they decided his life was more important than his job. His dad said, "We figured the worse case would be that he'd have to find another job. But if he lost his life, there'd be no second chance." During the conversation, the boss told the dad that he already knew there was a problem and agreed to write a letter of support that the family could read during the intervention. That letter from the boss was a powerful tool for the family. If you can get a letter from the alcoholic's employer, you're almost guaranteed the alcoholic will agree to treatment.

We've also worked with families who decide not to contact the workplace, and they take a risk, too. When a job issue is left hanging unresolved, plan for the alcoholic to use it as an opportunity to avoid treatment. Take the time to investigate your options. Not all companies have clear-cut policies or EAPs. If you investigate the workplace and find little or no guidance, you'll have to evaluate your situation and make a decision based on the best judgment of the intervention team as a whole.

Finalizing Your Team

Everyone should be trained and prepared before the intervention. Latecomers will not be prepared unless you bring them up to speed; it is far easier and more expedient if you finalize your team before you begin planning and rehearsing the intervention.

A good rule of thumb is to have no fewer than three people on your team and no more than eight. If you have fewer than three, you no longer have a group. For all purposes, it's a one-on-one confrontation with the alcoholic, which rarely works. If you have more than eight people, the intervention takes too long and can cause sensory overload for the alcoholic. We don't want to lose the alcoholic by talking his ear off. Strike a balance. More is not always better.

Of course, there are always exceptions to every rule, and we have to discuss those as well. We worked with a large, close-knit family who wanted to intervene on their son, who was addicted to alcohol and prescription opiates, or pain pills. They insisted that ten people participate in the intervention because each person was intensely significant in their son's life. We did the intervention with all ten people, but we compromised by asking everyone to shorten the letters they would read to the alcoholic. By doing so, we didn't overwhelm the son.

Sometimes a friend or relative would like to attend the intervention but cannot. She may have health problems, live too far away, or have important plans that conflict with the date of the intervention. Whatever the reason, a person can participate without being present by writing a letter and asking another family member to read it during the intervention. We do this frequently, and it works very well. While you're building your team, tell the person who can't attend that she can still participate. She will need to learn about intervention along with the rest of the team, but she doesn't have to be present to do it.

Sometimes a person you really want on your team doesn't want to get involved. He may be uncomfortable with the idea of intervention or too angry at the addict. We've found that many people mistakenly believe intervention is about beating up on the addict. The media has been known to misrepresent intervention, and word of mouth has carried the wrong message far and wide. Many times, when they learn the intervention is performed with love and the addict's dignity is preserved, reluctant family members agree to participate. Sometimes it takes more information.

If you have a family member who is very reluctant, yet very important to the intervention, ask him or her to participate in the planning and rehearsal stages before making a final decision. Going through the rehearsal is exactly like doing an intervention except the addict is not present. Having this full experience helps many people decide to participate. If they still feel they do not want a part in the intervention, then they should not attend. While it is reasonable to ask people to learn about intervention before making a decision, in the end they must make up their own mind. Anyone attending an intervention under duress weakens the intervention process.

One last word about your team. If a team member can't attend the rehearsal, he can't attend the intervention. In rare exceptions, we've had team members attend the rehearsal over the phone. One time, the wife of the alcoholic was driving from out-of-town with the alcoholic and couldn't attend the rehearsal without tipping him off. But she could get to a phone long enough to go through the rehearsal with the rest of the family. Whatever the circumstances, rehearsal attendance is not optional.

Becoming Aware of the Influence of the Group

Everyone who comes to an intervention has some degree of influence with the alcoholic. Past arguments and disagreements aside, these are people the alcoholic loves and respects most in his life.

Many people discount the power of their influence. We hear people say things like, "You don't know Frank. He's not about to listen to anybody." After all, this has been their past experience with the alcoholic. They've tried to talk to him—begged, pleaded, and bargained—but the alcoholic remained unmoved.

As part of a group, the influence of each person is more powerful than if they stood alone. A person who appears to have little power over the situation may have tremendous influence in an intervention. A recent experience of ours is the perfect example. We were conducting an intervention, and as the letters were read, the alcoholic wasn't showing any signs of emotion. We planned to have his fourteen-year-old daughter read her letter last. When her turn came, she paused and said nothing for what seemed like an eternity. In the silence that filled the room, all of our hearts raced faster. Finally, she looked at her father with tears in her eyes and a wonderful smile. She said, "Daddy, I love you so much!" Instantly, the man's eyes filled with tears, and he began to cry openly. The room was choked with emotion. Then his daughter cried, "I just want my Daddy back." Everyone started to sob, and our man of stone melted before the plea of his young daughter. She ran into his arms and hugged him. He immediately promised to get the help he needed. Never underestimate the influence of love.

Later, as you begin working on your letters, consider the effect of influence when deciding in what order people will read their letters. Ending with someone possessing extraordinary emotional influence, such as a child or an aging parent, can have a powerful impact.

We've heard it said that ultimately it is grace that breaks through an alcoholic's denial. We can't predict at what moment or with what word we will touch the alcoholic's heart. Our job is to be an instrument of love. We can never know in advance how things will work out, but we can do our best.

Understanding the Role of Leverage

Some people in the alcoholic's life carry enough weight or leverage to dispense consequences if the alcoholic chooses to continue drinking. Leverage is never a threat or a punishment. It is the refusal to continue enabling the alcoholic.

A boss has leverage over an employee. He can stipulate that the alcoholic go to treatment to keep his job. If the boss is present at the intervention, he or she may never have to spell out the consequences of job loss to the alcoholic. The boss's presence alone speaks volumes. The alcoholic may say, "So I guess I have to go along with this treatment if I want to keep my job."

If the boss doesn't attend, but writes a letter to be read at the intervention, he might say, "Maria, you're an important part of our team. We value you. But you need to accept help for your alcoholism before you return to work. We're here to support you in that decision."

If Maria doesn't go to treatment, she must accept responsibility for losing her job. She made the decision that led to her dismissal. The alcoholic always has a choice, but some choices come with negative consequences. Using leverage causes adversity in the alcoholic's life. Bill Wilson, co-founder of Alcoholics Anonymous, wrote: "Someone once remarked that pain is the touchstone of spiritual progress. How heartily we of Alcoholics Anonymous can agree with him, for we know that the pains of alcoholism had to come before sobriety, and emotional turmoil before serenity."

A spouse has leverage, because he or she can choose to ask for a separation or divorce if the alcoholic doesn't accept help. A wife might say to her husband: "Jack, your alcoholism has taken a terrible toll on our marriage and our children. My choice is to save our marriage. I love you. But if you won't accept help for yourself, I am prepared to put the welfare of our children first. I can't continue to raise our beautiful children in an alcoholic household. If you choose alcohol as the most important relationship in your life, I cannot stand by you under those circumstances."

Parents supporting or housing adult children who are alcoholics have leverage. We've worked with parents who support the alcoholic in grand style—paying the rent or mortgage, buying a condominium or house outright, covering the car payments and insurance, bankrolling one failed business venture after another, and providing spending money. No self-respecting alcoholic would give up so much just to get sober. Think of it this way: If your refrigerator, freezer, and cupboards are plumb full of food, why would you go to the grocery store? If an alcoholic has all his addiction needs covered, why get sober?

Parents use their leverage when they tell an adult child he will be financially cut off if he chooses alcohol and other drugs over treatment. This is very difficult for parents, because playing the role of caretaker is comfortable and natural. Even if the alcoholic is forty-two years old, the parents may react emotionally as if he were a child. There is an unspoken agreement between the parents and the alcoholic: The parents continue to act as caretakers as long as the alcoholic acts irresponsibly; the alcoholic continues to act irresponsibly as long as the parents take care of him. Using leverage puts an end to that agreement and sets up a new expectation—"We love you, but it's time for you to grow up."

Leverage can come from sources outside the family. If the alcoholic is arrested for driving under the influence, the court may mandate treatment. We recently had a call from a mother who was unable to control her seventeen-year-old daughter. The girl had been in trouble with the police and was skipping school. She was addicted to illegal drugs and running off with a twenty-four-year-old boyfriend who was her supplier. The girl was on probation so we advised the mother to contact the probation officer and bring the girl into court. As is usual in these cases, the judge offered the alternative of treatment instead of juvenile detention. The daughter quickly agreed. The boyfriend disappeared when he learned the parents weren't afraid to use the criminal justice system.

Sometimes leverage is more subtle. A daughter may tell her mother she'll no longer bring her family home for holidays because she refuses to subject herself and her children to the drinking. A grandmother may be told she can no longer baby-sit the grandchildren as long as she is addicted to Valium. A best friend may say he's willing to help in any way if the goal is sobriety, but he refuses to bail the alcoholic out of jail again, lend him money, or listen to his drunken tales of woe.

We know three sisters who shop and go to lunch with their mother every Saturday. It is the highlight of their mother's week. During an intervention on their mother, they were prepared to tell her there would be no more Saturday lunches if she chose alcohol over recovery. Sometimes leverage is withdrawing from the relationship. Again, this is not a punishment. It is saying, "If you choose to stay sick, I will no longer pretend everything is all right. Your alcoholism causes me to suffer, too. I need to start taking care of myself."

The alcoholic instinctively knows who in the room has leverage. We have seen alcoholics size up a situation in a matter of seconds and, calculating the sum of the leverage in the room, readily agree to help. If it is possible for you to involve someone who has heavy leverage, you are well advised to do so.

Not everyone chooses to use the leverage they have, and some people have no leverage to use. We'll talk more about this when we discuss bottom lines. For now, take an inventory of your team's leverage. Turn to the planner in section 6.

What Do You Need to Know?

An intervention team needs to work together. Each person should read or listen to the same information so the group can easily discuss what they are learning, answer questions, and settle differing opinions. If everybody is getting their information from a different source, sharing information can be clumsy and confusing.

If your team uses this book as a training tool, each person should become familiar with the Tools section. You will find a planner to help you compile and organize information, and a checklist to keep you on track. We've put together brainstorming segments to give you a head start when it comes to thinking up possible objections, writing your letter to the alcoholic, and evaluating a treatment center. We offer resources guiding you to the best books, support groups, and Web sites. If the entire group uses the Tools section, the group will move ahead in an organized and focused fashion. As you go through the sections of the book, we'll refer you to the Tools section as you need it.

You can begin by asking everyone on the team to read this book. Most of us are procrastinators at heart, so set a date when everyone will meet to discuss the steps needed to prepare for the intervention. If people are scattered across the country, meet over the phone.

During your meeting, select a *detail person*. Choose someone who is organized and willing to act as a liaison between team members. The detail person's two most important jobs are to keep communications flowing and to compile information. Likewise, the two most important tools are the planner and the checklist in section 6. The detail person serves the team rather than manages it.

Once your team meets, begin collecting information. Turn to the planner and fill in as much information as you can. If the team doesn't have all the answers during your first meeting, ask who can find the answers. Once the answers are found, give the information to the detail person.

List the tasks that need to be completed and ask for volunteers. As each person completes his or her task, let the detail person know, so he or she can check off these tasks on the checklist. All information should eventually find its way to the detail person so nothing gets lost in the shuffle. Record everything in the planner; don't rely on memory.

Think of intervention as a project—perhaps the most important project you'll ever work on. Intervention isn't complicated, but it requires knowledge and careful preparation. We've had calls from families telling us they're going to intervene on a relative the next day and plan to figure it out as they go along. That's how interventions fail. First learn what you need to know. Then plan and prepare.

The most important thing your team can do is work together and stay on the same track. The whole team participates in the preparation and planning. Don't take any shortcuts. Put in the work, and you'll be in the best possible position for success.

Using the Planner

When you begin an important project, what's the first thing you do? Plan, of course. Even baking a cake requires a plan. Every recipe is, after all, a plan. You're given a list of ingredients and the exact quantities you'll need. If you toss the recipe aside and throw a random amount of flour, sugar, water, eggs, and oil in a pan and bake your cake at whatever temperature you feel like using, you won't win any blue ribbons at the state fair. Without a plan, you'll end up with a flop.

Intervention success comes with careful planning. There is a specific recipe to follow when doing an intervention, and the planner in the Tools section helps you assemble the ingredients you'll need before you begin. Once you've selected your intervention team, start by listing their names and telephone numbers in the planner. Include cellular phone and pager numbers. This gives you a one-stop resource when you have to sit down and call team members. It's the small annoyances, like not finding a telephone number when you need it, that can create frustrations at a time when nerves already are taut.

Continue to follow along with the planner just as you would a cake recipe. Next, the planner asks you for the dates and times of the intervention and the rehearsal. Work with your team to set a schedule for the intervention. This may require some juggling, but unless something is very important, most people can make reasonable adjustments in their schedules. The reason you set your dates and times early in the planning stage is that you are going to work backwards from your intervention date. If you set your date and time for the intervention on October 3 at ten o'clock, all of your planning starts there and moves backward: "We'll assemble at Mom and Dad's house at nine on the morning of the intervention to give us an hour before the alcoholic's arrival; we'll have the rehearsal on October 2 at six-thirty; set an appointment at the treatment center for October 3 at eleven-thirty." Having a date, time, and location sets the wheels in motion.

Next, you determine the financial details. This will have everything to do with how you proceed in locating treatment for the alcoholic. If the alcoholic has health insurance, the insurance company often dictates which facility it will cover and what steps you must take to precertify the alcoholic. In other words, you must contact the insurance company and follow its rules, or it may not cover the costs of treatment. Treatment centers can be very helpful when investigating insurance coverage. Using computers, they can look up a policy and tell you all the particulars, including copays, average number of days covered, precertification requirements, and which treatment centers the insurance company uses.

Don't rely on written policy guidelines when determining the number of days of treatment the insurance company will cover. It is not unusual for a policy to say it will cover thirty days of inpatient treatment and then certify only seven days, for example. Most insurance companies use "medical necessity" as the criterion for determining the length of inpatient treatment. This means that once the alcoholic or addict is physically stable—detoxed from the drug—the insurance company will no longer pay for inpatient treatment. Alcoholics and addicts requiring intensive support, but who are physically stable, will have difficulty convincing insurance companies to pay for extra days in inpatient treatment. Families are often left to believe it was the treatment center's decision to discharge the patient.

A family we worked with was furious when their thirty-nine-year-old son, suffering from late-stage alcoholism, was discharged after six days of inpatient care. Unknowingly, the family blamed the treatment center for discharging him too soon because the insurance company assured them that their son had thirty days of coverage. With some investigation, we learned the insurance company declined to pay for more than six days of inpatient treatment. The treatment center appealed the decision, but the insurance company denied the appeal. The alcoholic was discharged from treatment and, as predicted by the treatment staff, drank soon after his release. Ask the admissions staff at the treatment center to estimate how many days of treatment the insurance company will provide and have a contingency plan to provide additional support if necessary. We'll give you some direction on how to do this later. For now, get a clear picture of the financial details and write them down.

If the alcoholic does not have insurance, explore other options for paying for treatment. If the family decides to pay for treatment privately, ask if the treatment center offers a discount for private payment. In addition, inquire about patient aid. Many treatment centers raise funds to help pay a percentage of the costs for people without insurance. If there is no family money available for treatment, look for other funding sources. Call a local treatment center for suggestions. They may know of agencies in your local area that can help.

Once you've narrowed down your treatment center choices, ask the staff about the admissions policies. They will explain what you need to do before the alcoholic can be admitted. Sometimes the admissions staff requests that the alcoholic call for a pre-intake interview. Do not assume the admissions staff is familiar with intervention. Explain that you are planning an intervention and why it's impossible to ask the alcoholic to call the treatment center. Suggest that a family member provide the pre-intake information. Then, as a group, the team can compile the facts essential to the pre-intake interview and record them in the planner. Each member of your team has seen a different part of the alcoholic's life, so use the collective experiences of the group to get the most complete picture. By completing this section of the planner, you should be able to answer all of the pre-intake questions.

Use the planner from the start. Laying the groundwork prepares you for each step to come. As Plato wrote in the *New Republic,* "The beginning is the most important part of the work."

Keeping Tabs on Your Progress

You will always know what you've done and what you haven't done by faithfully using the checklist in the Tools section. The checklist is an indispensable tool for the detail person, but every member of the team will do well to monitor the progress of the intervention preparations.

Many of us think we can rely on our memories, but intervention requires attending to too many details. Consider planning a wedding without a checklist. If you get 95 percent of the details right it won't be of much comfort as you try to explain why there are no flowers because you forgot to confirm the order with the florist. Planning an intervention isn't as complicated as planning a wedding, but every little detail is important. If the addict agrees to treatment and no one packed a suitcase, the time it takes to pack the suitcase could give the addict enough time to think up a reason not to go.

The checklist can be used as a resource for assigning tasks. Read through the tasks with the entire team. The detail person can write the name of the responsible person next to each task on the checklist. Team members can place an asterisk next to the tasks for which they volunteered. Some things on the checklist are completed by everyone on the team, such as writing a letter to the alcoholic and identifying objections the alcoholic may use to avoid going to treatment. As team members complete tasks, they should contact the detail person so he or she can check them off the master list.

When the team assembles for the rehearsal, the first thing you want to do is go over the checklist. If anything has not been done, this is your last chance. If there are problems, now's the time to straighten them out. The only tasks left unchecked should be ones that don't pertain to your intervention, such as making airline reservations when the treatment center is local.

The checklist gives you bare-bones information and this book provides the fat. Your success materializes from your preparation, not from half-measures and a wish for good luck. As Thomas Jefferson noted, "I find the harder I work, the more luck I seem to have."

Calling Treatment Centers and Asking Questions

Treatment centers are not created equal, so ask questions. Most people do not know what to look for when shopping for a treatment center and often make random choices. Choose programs that treat addiction as a primary disease and use the Twelve Steps of Alcoholics Anonymous. These programs are still considered the most effective.

If you stumble across someone who claims they have found the cure or a new way to treat the problem no one else has thought of before, be wary. People who come up with overly simple answers to complex problems make exciting promises, but upon closer examination, they don't have the experience or research to back themselves up. Quick fixes and easy promises lead to disappointments.

Talk to people who are active in Alcoholics Anonymous and Al-Anon. They can often give recommendations based on personal experiences with treatment centers. Use recommendations as a starting point. Since treatment centers can change over time, it is important to research each center for yourself.

Make an educated decision by evaluating treatment centers using the questions in the Tools section. Make sure you speak with a qualified staff member. Ask to talk with the program director, clinical staff, or someone in the admissions department who is familiar with the treatment program. Sometimes people working in admissions have a limited understanding of the program and cannot provide accurate information. Remember, you are the customer. Expect clear information about the services before you buy them.

Take the time to research treatment centers. If an insurance company gives you only one choice, research it anyway. If you think it's a bad choice, find out how you can contest the referral. It's difficult to get an alcoholic or addict into treatment in the first place. Once we do, we want them to have the best treatment possible.

Choosing a Date and Time

As you choose a date for the intervention, turn your attention to what works for the alcoholic. Selecting the right day, time, and place can determine the success of an intervention. By intervening at the wrong time, the intervention can fail.

The first and perhaps most important consideration is selecting a time when the addicted person is most likely to be sober. With this goal in mind, we usually schedule interventions early in the morning and shortly after the alcoholic awakens. If an alcoholic is not sober for the intervention, it's almost impossible to reach him emotionally. Alcohol and other mood-altering drugs block emotional intimacy and alter moods. While high, people's feelings and reactions are dominated by the drug. When an alcoholic is even slightly inebriated during an intervention, he is influenced by the drug—not his family. This forces the family to depend solely on leverage.

Sometimes the family will tell us the alcoholic is never sober. This is certainly true of late-stage alcoholics who drink around the clock to keep withdrawal symptoms at bay. In these circumstances, the alcoholic may get up every few hours during the night to drink. If this is what you are facing, select a time the person will have the least amount of alcohol in his system. He'll never be alcohol-free. Try to catch him when he's drinking his first eye-opener of the morning. Often, when we intervened on a round-the-clock drinker, we've had to let him take a drink before he'd agree to go to treatment.

Another strategy is to have the intervention at a place where the alcoholic won't drink. For example, we did an intervention on an alcoholic who drank all the time except when he was visiting his mother. He never touched a drop at his mother's house. The family planned a three-day visit with the mother over Memorial Day weekend. That Sunday morning we held the intervention. The alcoholic was cold sober and receptive to the family's expressions of love. He cried as everyone read their letters to him and agreed to go into treatment. Another intervention was done at the alcoholic's workplace because the family knew the alcoholic was most likely to be sober on the job. A supportive boss agreed to hold a confidential intervention in an unused conference room.

If your loved one is using drugs other than alcohol, it can be difficult to know if he is or isn't intoxicated. Again, early in the morning is usually the best time to intervene. Afternoons and evenings are times when the addict is most likely to be high. If the drug is crack cocaine, the pattern of use is often *binge*—using large quantities of the drug for a prolonged period of time followed by periods of abstinence. Crack addicts will run out of money, exhaust themselves, become physically ill from lack of sleep and food, all of which will force them to stop using crack long enough to recuperate. In these cases, be flexible enough to intervene when the addict is coming off a binge. Make sure he's not using alcohol to come down from the crack at the time of the intervention.

If the drug is heroin or other opiates, the addict usually will have the drug in his system all the time. Marijuana use is harder to predict. The patterns of use can vary widely like those of alcohol. Some marijuana addicts light up as soon as they open their eyes in the morning. If that's the case, look for opportunities when the addict won't be smoking pot. That may be during a holiday at the folks' house or a time when he's expecting to get together with nieces and nephews. You have to be creative in these situations.

Once making the decision to intervene, families usually want to move ahead quickly. But don't sacrifice smart planning for speed. However, if you believe the alcoholic or addict is in immediate danger of hurting himself or someone else, by all means move as quickly as possible. We've done interventions twenty-four hours after first being contacted by a family. If you need to proceed this quickly, contact a professional interventionist right now. There is no way you can properly prepare for an intervention in a day or two without using a professional. Most families coordinating an intervention on their own take one to two weeks to do so.

A man wanted to intervene on his alcoholic wife when she suddenly decided to go on the wagon. We told him he couldn't intervene unless she started drinking again. Don't ever intervene on someone who is abstaining at the moment. She'll say, "Hey, I'm sober. I'm not drinking anymore." What can you say to that? Wait for the alcoholic to begin drinking again before you intervene.

Occasionally families want to intervene right before an important function or celebration in the alcoholic's life. If you are planning to ask a father, for instance, to miss his daughter's wedding to go into treatment, you'll probably lose the battle. However, we helped intervene on a man just before his cousin's wedding. The cousin wrote a letter for the intervention saying the best wedding present the alcoholic could give him was to go into treatment. If you believe the alcoholic is in extreme danger, don't let anything stand in your way of moving quickly. However, if you feel it is safe to wait a few days or a week, let the alcoholic attend the big event before the intervention.

Choosing a Place

Besides dates and times, there are guidelines to follow when selecting a location for intervention. Choose a residence other than the addict's home. When you hold the intervention at a neutral location, the addict is not as empowered as he may be on his own turf. We like to choose the homes of family members or friends that the alcoholic holds in high regard. The addict is naturally going to be on her best behavior in such an environment. Never intervene on an addict in a public place, such as a restaurant.

When you've selected a location, be sure you devise a plausible reason for the alcoholic to show up for the intervention. Remember, she mustn't know she's going to be intervened upon. Intervention is a bit like a surprise party. If the birthday girl is tipped off beforehand or doesn't show up at all, your surprise party goes bust. When selecting a location, think of ways to get the alcoholic there. Families do this in a variety of ways.

One family, intervening on their grandmother, invited her to an early afternoon birthday celebration for her adult grandson. After successfully intervening on the grandmother, they cut the cake and sang "Happy Birthday." Another family asked an alcoholic uncle to show up early Sunday morning to baby-sit his nephews. They knew he'd show up sober and on time. Another alcoholic was summoned by his boss for a meeting, and when he arrived his entire family was present. In another case, a man set up a golf date with the alcoholic brother, his father, and his best friend. He said he'd pick the brother up, and everyone was meeting at the dad's house first. Usually, parents, grandparents, or a best friend have enough influence to successfully summon the alcoholic for a visit.

You know the relationships in your family and what will work best. Make these decisions as a team. If you can arrange for someone to drive the alcoholic to the intervention location, all the better. Do what you can to ensure that the alcoholic shows up.

There are times when it is impossible to get the alcoholic to go anywhere, and you'll have to use her home for the intervention. If the alcoholic lives with someone else, such as a spouse or a roommate, that person is key in making these arrangements. They know the alcoholic's day-to-day habits best. Before the intervention, everybody other than the person who lives with the alcoholic meets at another location, such as at a parking lot or landmark close to the alcoholic's home. Once everyone has arrived, drive to the alcoholic's house caravan-style. This way, everybody arrives at the same time and walks into the house together. Have a cell phone with you so the alcoholic's spouse or roommate can contact you with last-minute directions. He or she may ask you to wait a little longer before arriving because the alcoholic is in the shower.

If no one lives with the alcoholic, you can make a surprise visit or a family member can call ahead saying they'll be stopping by. One family used an addict's eviction as a reason to show up at his apartment. They called and asked if they could help him move his furniture into storage. The family arrived together, successfully intervened, drove him to treatment, and returned to the apartment to move his belongings out, just as they'd promised.

What if the addict is living on the street, in his car, or in a flop house? For one intervention, a good friend found the alcoholic living out of his car and invited him home for dinner. One homeless addict would only respond to his grandmother, so a sister found him and told him the grandmother wanted to see him right away. He got in the sister's car and went with her to the grandmother's house where the rest of the family was waiting.

Sometimes, when the addict is homeless, we set up a small mobile intervention team. It might be a group of three or four people who carry a lot of influence with the addict. The mobile team is trained and ready to take action when an opportunity presents itself. This requires flexibility on their part. The mobile team goes to the addict wherever he might be. If he's in jail, they show up at the precinct. If he's living in a flop house, they contact him there. They may even track down his car and try to catch him sleeping in it. When they do locate him, they proceed with the intervention just as they would in any other setting.

When somebody is homeless, the family has less and less influence and leverage over him or her. However, we've seen success stories in the most extreme circumstances and discourage anyone from labeling an addicted person as hopeless. The co-author of this book is a perfect example. His dad had found him in a flop house on the very day he was planning to commit suicide. The family intervened, got him into treatment, and Jeff's been sober ever since.

It's always a good idea to get input from the entire group before you choose the date, time, and location for the intervention. The more ideas you generate, the better. There's always a chance the alcoholic won't show up. If this happens, don't fret. Put your heads together and come up with another plan. Remember that intervention is a process, not an event.

Selecting a Chairperson

The chairperson is a combination of host, guide, and spokesperson during the intervention. He or she is the relative, friend, or colleague who is most respected by the alcoholic. This person is someone the alcoholic would not want to disappoint and would most likely turn to in his hour of greatest need. Most families know right away who the chairperson should be.

The chairperson isn't always the one who is emotionally closest to the alcoholic. Close emotional relationships can often be the most tumultuous. Someone having a stormy relationship with the alcoholic probably won't be appropriate as the chairperson.

We worked with a woman who intervened on her husband. He was incorrigible, unemployed, and she suspected he had a girlfriend on the side. He didn't seem to care about the marriage, and the wife had little influence or leverage on him. What made all the difference was selecting the alcoholic's father as the chairperson. The father commanded great respect from all his children. The mere idea of disappointing the father was unimaginable in this family. The alcoholic, greeted by his father at the door, was receptive during the intervention and agreed to accept help. Going against his father's wishes was a more painful idea to him than going to treatment.

Another family asked a seventy-five-year-old uncle to be the chairperson. He didn't have the closest relationship to the alcoholic, but the alcoholic was most likely to respond to him in a positive and respectful manner. Yet another family chose an older sister who'd been in recovery herself for several years; another selected a brother who'd always been steady and calm in his dealings with the alcoholic. Other good choices may include a friend, mentor, pastor, priest, or rabbi. Select the person who best fits the profile for a chairperson.

During an intervention, no one talks off the top of his head. Everyone writes a letter to read to the alcoholic, which we'll discuss later in this section, and no one says anything other than what is written on his piece of paper, except the chairperson. The chairperson greets the alcoholic, seats the alcoholic, makes an opening statement, asks the team to read their letters, answers any objections, asks the alcoholic to accept help, and makes the closing remarks. This is all done using very few words. Later in the book, we've provided a script for the chairperson to use as a guide. We will prepare the chairperson for any number of responses from the alcoholic, but alcoholics typically do not act out during interventions.

The team must never get into a free-for-all debate with the alcoholic. If you do this, the alcoholic will take the power away from the group and the intervention will fail. Team members read their letters and say nothing else. The chairperson is the singular voice for everything else that needs to be said. Hearing one constant voice disarms the alcoholic and makes it impossible for him to bait or manipulate the group. If the alcoholic challenges someone in the group, that person doesn't respond—the chairperson does. If you have the urge to speak up during the intervention, don't. Trust your chairperson to do his or her job. If arguing with the alcoholic worked, it would have done so already. Don't fall into old patterns during the intervention.

If the alcoholic has alienated everybody in his life, and there's no one who can fill the role of chairperson, use a professional interventionist. Interventionists can play the role of chairperson

Do You Need a Professional Interventionist?

Before intervention, families were powerless in the face of addiction. They had no option but to watch the alcoholic spiral downward out of control. Then, in the 1960s, a minister named Dr. Vernon Johnson and his congregation developed a way families could intervene on an addicted loved one. The intervention techniques were designed for families to use and were not part of the professional world. Since that time, a new profession has sprung up based on Dr. Johnson's work—the interventionist.

Once intervention became professionalized, there has been an ongoing debate whether or not families should proceed without a professional interventionist present. We believe that most families who take the time to educate themselves, follow all the guidelines, and thoroughly prepare for an intervention are not obligated to hire a professional. We've had conversations with many families who have competently performed an intervention without an interventionist. In his book *Intervention*, Johnson writes, "Anyone who sincerely wants to help, can help. Chances are you're quite capable of doing an intervention without the assistance of a qualified professional. However, if you feel the need for such assistance, you should seek it."

Many families prefer to have an interventionist present. They feel more comfortable working with a professional; other families feel confident proceeding without one. You should make the decision based on the feelings of your team as a whole.

Costs for an interventionist can range anywhere from five hundred to twenty-five hundred dollars or more. Oftentimes, there is no interventionist available locally. If you bring an interventionist in from out of town, expect to pay for travel expenses and accommodations.

From time to time, the alcoholic may be facing problems that go beyond chemical dependency, making intervention more complicated. In these cases, a professional interventionist should be present for the rehearsal and the intervention. Dr. Johnson described four special circumstances when a family should consider using a professional: (1) when there is a history of mental illness; (2) behavior has been abusive or violent; (3) there has been a long-lasting, deep depression; or (4) you suspect several drugs are being used, but you can't verify which drugs.

In addition, we would suggest three more reasons to hire a professional: (1) the alcoholic has had several previous treatments followed by relapse; (2) there is a history of suicide attempts or recent threats of suicide; and (3) family relationships have greatly deteriorated with the alcoholic and there is no one appropriate for the chairperson role.

If none of the above special circumstances fit your situation but you'd feel more comfortable with a professional, call a local treatment center for a referral. If there is no treatment center in your hometown, call a nearby city, or call Hazelden in Minnesota, at 800-257-7810, Hanley-Hazelden in Florida at 800-444-7008, or the Betty Ford Center in California at 800-854-9211. Any of these centers can give you the name of an interventionist who will travel anywhere in the country to do interventions.

Choosing Inpatient over Outpatient Treatment

Following an intervention, we prefer to send the alcoholic to an inpatient treatment program. An alcoholic who has been through an intervention needs the support of residential care. During the intervention, the family breaks through denial and the alcoholic sees the light—but only for a short time. The disease will take control again and denial will spring back into place.

All alcoholics experience anger while in treatment, but after an intervention, anger may rise up faster and with more intensity. When this happens, we want the alcoholic in a residential program staffed by counselors ready to pick up where the family left off. Two of the primary jobs of alcohol and drug counselors are to continue breaking through the denial and to help the alcoholic work through anger.

Since the onset of managed care, many insurance policies pay only for outpatient treatment. They certify the lowest level of care, and they reassess the alcoholic's needs at that point. How would we respond if a woman with breast cancer was first treated at the lowest level of care? Would it be acceptable to us to deny her surgery until she first failed at radiation? Of course not. The same holds true for chemical dependency. Start with the support of a more intensive treatment program, and move to less intensive care when the alcoholic is ready. When an alcoholic fails in treatment and starts drinking again, it's not easy for a family to convince him to go back into treatment. With each relapse, there is a risk we will lose the alcoholic.

In 1991, MEDSTAT, a company that specializes in health services research, completed a study of three million people. Among other things, they studied the people who entered treatment for chemical dependency and documented what percentage relapsed within the first year. MEDSTAT found there was a direct correlation between the rate of relapse and the length of stay in an inpatient treatment setting. Alcoholics who stayed in treatment longer had a lower rate of relapse. Forty-eight percent of the people who received one to seven days of treatment relapsed, whereas only 21 percent relapsed after twenty-two to thirty days of treatment.

Since insurance companies now primarily cover outpatient treatment, hundreds of residential treatment centers around the country have closed their doors. If you can't find inpatient treatment in your hometown, call nearby cities. If you still don't find what you are looking for, we can recommend several treatment programs that have long-standing reputations. All of the following treatment centers are nonprofits. They base their treatment programs on the Twelve Steps of Alcoholics Anonymous, employ certified alcohol and drug counselors, have medical staff, and offer family programs. Evaluate these centers for yourself using the questions in the Tools section and determine which offers the best program for your loved one.

- The Betty Ford Center, Rancho Mirage, California
  800-854-9211
  www.bettyfordcenter.org

  People often believe the Betty Ford Center is only for celebrities and is more expensive than comparable centers. Neither is true. If the alcoholic doesn't have insurance and has limited financial resources, ask about the scholarship program.

- Brighton Hospital, Brighton, Michigan
  888-215-2700
  www.brightonhospital.org

  Founded in 1950, Brighton has a long tradition of treating alcoholics and offers a separate track for heroin and cocaine addicts. Brighton provides a special treatment program for health professionals, a facility for adolescents, and treatment for addicted people with other mental health problems.

- Caron Foundation, Wernersville, Pennsylvania
  800-678-2332
  www.caron.org

  Founded in 1959 at a historic resort hotel, Caron provides detoxification and stabilization, residential treatment for adults and adolescents, aftercare, family counseling, and codependency treatment. Programs are based on the Twelve Step philosophy. See their Web site for a full menu of services.

- Crossroads Centre, Antigua, West Indies
  268-562-0035
  www.crossroadsantigua.org

  Situated on ten acres on Antigua's coast, the facility accommodates up to thirty-six clients. The Crossroads Centre offers medical detoxification, individual and group therapy, exercise therapy, massage therapy, Twelve Step meetings, lectures and discussion groups, and an emphasis on ongoing recovery. See their Web site for travel information.

- Father Martin's Ashley, Havre de Grace, Maryland
  800-799-4673
  www.fathermartinsashley.com

  This nondenominational center for the treatment of alcoholics and chemically addicted people is situated on forty-three acres overlooking Chesapeake Bay in Maryland. It provides a relapse program for people who have had previous treatments and are unable to stay sober.

- Hazelden Foundation, Center City, Minnesota
  800-257-7810
  www.hazelden.org

    Founded fifty years ago, this program is internationally known and considered the pioneer of modern treatment. They have another center in West Palm Beach, Florida, and an adolescent center in Plymouth, Minnesota. Review the array of services on the Web site. If you have no insurance and limited financial resources, ask to speak to a financial case manager for information about the patient aid fund.

If inpatient treatment isn't possible, make an appointment with the outpatient counselor for the day of the intervention. The counselor will do an assessment of the alcoholic's needs and make treatment recommendations. Ask the alcoholic to follow all recommendations. If a spouse or roommate is worried the alcoholic may return home and lash out in anger, arrange for one or two people from the intervention team to spend the night. Refuse to engage in debates or arguments. If the alcoholic acts out in an inappropriate manner, spend the night with a relative or friend.

Finding Low-Cost or No-Cost Treatment

It doesn't do any good to intervene on an alcoholic and then have nowhere to go for treatment. If the alcoholic doesn't have insurance and has little or no money for treatment, there are several options. With a few phone calls, most people find public funding or a low-cost or no-cost treatment program. Keep in mind as you begin making phone calls that some of the people staffing state agencies and publicly funded treatment centers are overworked and have very little time to talk. Prepare your questions before you call, stay focused on getting information on finding no-cost or low-cost treatment, and be brief when describing the alcoholic's problems. Be persistent. If the person you're talking with can't help you, ask them to refer you to someone else.

Funding for treatment is often available at the local, county, and state levels, but policies can vary. Some agencies require the addict to call personally, come in for an evaluation, and wait a week or two before funding is granted. If you come up against similar policies, you can call treatment centers and ask if they know of programs that treat people with no funding. Or you can ask the alcoholic to make the required call to the agency at the end of the intervention and have someone from the intervention team accompany him to the evaluation.

A friend of ours called us about her cousin who was dying of alcoholism. Insurance covered a one-week stay at a treatment center then discharged her. She went to a few Alcoholics Anonymous meetings, but started drinking again. She was a late-stage alcoholic who needed more than a week of intensive treatment, but didn't have the money to pay once her insurance ran out. We called around to different treatment centers in several cities in the alcoholic's home state. Eventually we were referred to a state-funded treatment center that provided the alcoholic with three months of treatment at no cost.

The Salvation Army provides excellent treatment programs in many cities throughout the country. Some of the centers accept people on a first-come, first-served basis only, and beds aren't guaranteed or reserved. Call about admissions policies to see if they will fit your needs.

Low-Cost Recovery Programs

There are some recovery programs around the country that provide impressive care in beautiful settings at a very low cost. You may have to buy an airline ticket, but this is a worthwhile option if you have some financial resources. We've visited three low-cost facilities that we can personally recommend.

The first is Sundown M Ranch in Selah, Washington. The facility is set on thirty acres at the entrance of the Yakima River Canyon and has separate programs for adults and adolescents. It offers overnight accommodations for families attending the family program. It has a medical doctor on site as well as certified counselors. As of this writing, a twenty-eight-day stay for an adolescent costs less than five thousand dollars; a twenty-eight-day stay for an adult costs less than four thousand dollars. Family counseling is included in the cost of treatment. You can call 800-326-7444 for more information or visit their Web site at **www.sundown.org**. Ask about the free video.

Founded in 1940, High Watch Farm in Kent, Connecticut, is situated on 200 acres in the Connecticut Berkshires. High Watch Farm offers a nonmedical approach and does not staff counselors or social workers. They depend on practitioners working with the Twelve Steps of Alcoholics Anonymous, and everyone from the dishwasher to the president is recovering. They require seventy-two hours of abstinence prior to admission because they do not offer a medical detox facility. This is an adult-only program. Go to their Web site at **www.highwatchfarm.org** or call 860-927-3772. A month-long stay costs less than three thousand dollars.

The Retreat at Upland Farms is twenty miles west of downtown Minneapolis, Minnesota. Located on 170 acres of rolling hills on the Upland Farm Estates, The Retreat describes itself as a nonclinical, self-help approach to the problem of alcohol and drug abuse. The program is grounded in the spiritual principles of Alcoholics Anonymous and provides a safe and supportive environment to practice the Alcoholics Anonymous principles. They do not offer medical detox services and require the chemically dependent person to be medically stable prior to admission. Visit their Web site at **www.theretreat.com** or call 952-446-9283. A month-long stay at The Retreat costs less than three thousand dollars.

Not all alcoholics and addicts go to treatment. Many get sober by going directly into Alcoholics Anonymous or Narcotics Anonymous. Treatment prepares people for recovery, but recovery happens in Alcoholics Anonymous or Narcotics Anonymous. Some people need the initial support of treatment to give them a good running start at sobriety. But if you find yourself in the position of having absolutely no treatment options available to you, you can ask the alcoholic to go to Alcoholics Anonymous or Narcotics Anonymous. At the end of the intervention say, "We'd like you to go to Alcoholics Anonymous (Narcotics Anonymous), get an Alcoholics Anonymous (Narcotics Anonymous) sponsor, and work the Twelve Steps." Call Alcoholics Anonymous and request a schedule of local meetings so you can give it to the alcoholic after the intervention.

Families often say, "She'll never go to Alcoholics Anonymous.

She hates Alcoholics Anonymous." Most alcoholics, walking through the doors of Alcoholics Anonymous for the first time, don't like it. But after working a good program of recovery, they learn to love it. If the alcoholic objects, remind her that it's not about liking Alcoholics Anonymous, it's about needing it.

How many meetings a week are necessary? A good rule of thumb is to ask the alcoholic to go to the same number of meetings as the number of days she drinks every week. If she drinks every day, go to a meeting every day. Recovering alcoholics often recommend ninety meetings in ninety days. We'd suggest no less than four meetings per week for someone new to recovery.

Family members should not attend Alcoholics Anonymous meetings with the alcoholic, but attend a Twelve Step program for families. Often Al-Anon, Nar-Anon, and Families Anonymous meetings are scheduled at the same time and same place, but in different rooms from Alcoholics Anonymous and Narcotics Anonymous meetings.

Writing a Letter
to Your Addicted Loved One

During an intervention, emotions can run high. It is most effective if each person writes a letter to the alcoholic to read during the intervention. Letters prevent you from exploding into spontaneous anger or freezing up at the last moment.

When you begin your letter, think in terms of keeping it no shorter than one-half page and no longer than two pages. This doesn't mean squeezing three pages into two by using a tiny type size on your word processor. If you are using a typewriter or computer, your letter should be double-spaced and no longer than two pages. Be selective about what you will write. Believe us when we say the alcoholic knows what you're talking about without reminding him of every single detail.

Think of your letter as having three parts. First, begin with a message of love. The alcoholic needs to hear you speak from your heart. This may be the most important part of the letter. It's not enough to say "I love you" or "You're my best friend." Use the "who, what, where, when, how, and why" rule that journalists follow. The *who* is the alcoholic, but *what* about the alcoholic do you love or cherish? Talk about memories. *Where* you were; *when* it happened; and *how* you felt. Tell him *why* you love him. List the special qualities he possesses, the things you miss about him. Be specific, and speak with love first.

If the alcoholic has ever helped you when you were facing a

tough time, tell him how much that meant to you. A mother once told a son, "When your father died, you were there for me. You came over every day to keep me company, to fix things around the house, to give me a shoulder to cry on. If it hadn't been for you, I don't know how I would have gotten through that time."

A brother told his sister, "When I went through my divorce, you were there to keep me going. My world was falling apart, and it was your strength and optimism that got me through. Today I'm here for you." Accepting help can be difficult. If you can remind the alcoholic of a time when she helped you, it may be easier for her to take the help you are offering now.

Has the relationship you've had with the alcoholic been strained for so long you don't have much good to say about him? A wife once told us, "How can I write about loving him? I hate him!" We reminded her that you only feel "hate" when you still care about someone. When you don't care, you feel nothing. We suggested she think back on all the reasons she married him in the first place and write about those. If your relationship with the addict hasn't been the best, go back to a time when it was better.

The second section of the letter addresses the addiction. When you write this part of the letter, you must be vigilant against anger, judgment, and blame seeping in between the lines. No matter how angry you are with the alcoholic, leave the anger outside the door when you come in to do an intervention.

When you write your firsthand experience, be specific. A good example comes from a letter a woman wrote to her husband:

> Three Saturdays ago, you started drinking around noon.
> First it was beer, but then you switched to Jack Daniels.
> Your mood changed and, it seemed to me, everything I
> did irritated you. You ended up yelling at me at the top

of your voice in front of the kids. You took off in the car, screeching your tires on your way down the street. Darrell went into his bedroom and cried after you left. I worried all night that driving drunk you'd kill yourself or someone else. I was afraid every time the phone rang that it would be the police. The next morning when you came home, I was so angry I couldn't even speak to you. I gathered up the kids and left.

Notice how the wife avoided making judgmental statements? Even when she says *everything I did irritated you,* she qualified that statement by adding the words *it seemed to me.* In other words, she wasn't telling him what he was thinking, but what she was feeling. Don't try to guess what the alcoholic was thinking. Only report what he was doing.

When we say to use specific facts, it doesn't mean you must be cold or unemotional. You can report how you felt at the time. That's a fact, too. But don't let judgment, blame, or resentment sneak into your letter masquerading as truth. Test yourself by asking, "Am I trying to shame the alcoholic by saying this?" Intervention is no place for settling scores.

Here is a list of words that express uncomfortable feelings. Use them to communicate what you were feeling in a given situation. None are blaming words.

Angry	Hurt	Frustrated	Bewildered
Discouraged	Insignificant	Rejected	Confused
Helpless	Insecure	Reckless	Embarrassed
Anxious	Inadequate	Lonely	Miserable
Depressed	Ashamed	Guilty	Inferior
Worried	Afraid	Apathetic	Numb

The woman writing to her husband used the words *worried, afraid,* and *angry.* Again, her focus was on herself. These words explained how she felt. She didn't use extreme words like *tormented, terrified,* and *furious.* Those words imply blame.

Don't go too far into the past by digging up ancient history. We suggest sticking to the last six to twelve months. Families sometimes feel a certain incident that took place several years ago is so significant it must be mentioned. Other times, a person on the team has been separated from the alcoholic for a number of years and doesn't have recent experiences to draw from, but several older examples. Use the most recent or significant information available to you.

If a team member has never witnessed the alcoholic's drinking or drugging behavior, they can write something like this: "I've been living far away for a long time. You and I haven't seen much of each other except at Christmas. But for the last three or four years, Mom has called me to talk about how concerned she is about your drinking. She's confided in me, so I've worried, too. Alcoholism runs in our family. Uncle Art died of cirrhosis and our cousin Regina has been in recovery for five years now. I'm here today because I know alcoholism is a serious disease, and I don't want to lose you."

Those who say they've never witnessed the alcoholic's drinking often remember little things as they prepare for the intervention—slurred words during late night phone calls, conversations the alcoholic can't recall later on, repeated requests for loans, prescription pain pills missing from the medicine cabinet. Don't overlook the subtle ways your relative or friend's alcoholism has shown itself to you.

Write one to three examples of your firsthand experiences with the addiction, including failed past attempts at sobriety. If the addict has caused endless trouble, it is tempting to list everything. If you read a list of every single thing the alcoholic has done over the last year, you will sound blaming and judgmental. Detail is good, but being overly scrupulous is not. Keep it short.

A special note to spouses. Because yours is a uniquely intimate relationship with the alcoholic, you may have been exposed to behaviors too private to repeat during an intervention. If you were to do so, even as a factual statement, you would humiliate your wife or husband. Our first goal is to preserve the alcoholic's dignity, so keep highly intimate things out of your letter.

The third and last part to letter writing concerns the closing. Repeat here how much you care and how concerned you are. Then state your support of recovery and ask the alcoholic to accept help. This can usually be accomplished in one paragraph. You could write, "I can't imagine what life would be like without you. The pain would be unbearable for me. I don't want to lose you to this disease, and I am committed to do whatever it takes to help you get into recovery. I've taken the time to learn a lot about alcoholism, and I know you can get better with the help of others. Will you please accept the help we are offering you today? With love, your sister."

A few last words on writing your letter. Start your letter with a salutation, such as *Dear Dad* or *Dear Bill.* End it by referring to your relationship, such as *Your loving daughter, Kay.* You may think it silly to read your letter that way when you and the alcoholic are sitting in the same room. As silly as it might seem, it is more intimate and has a deeper emotional impact.

End your letter with a direct question asking the alcoholic to accept help. Specify that you are asking him to take immediate action by including words like *today* or *now.* The entire purpose of writing your letter is ultimately to come to this question, "Will you accept the help we're offering you today?" Everyone's letter should end with a similar question.

As you write, stay in the first person. Don't speak for the group. Instead of writing, *we all love you,* speak only for yourself. *I love you.* When you use *we* instead of *I,* you dilute the emotional power of your message. Only use *we* when you specifically want to refer to the intervention group, such as in your final question, "Will you accept the help *we* are offering you today?"

Letters Written for Real Interventions

Below are three letters that were read in actual interventions. All three are excellent examples of how to write an intervention letter. Changes have been made to protect the anonymity of the writers and the people being intervened on.

An adult daughter wrote the first letter to her father:

Dear Dad,

We don't talk about it ever, but I love you very much. I know you love me very much, and you are very proud of me. I wouldn't be where I am, or have what I have, if it weren't for you. You taught me that I need to learn how to take care of myself before I rely on anyone else to do it for me. You encouraged me and supported me in my career aspirations. This gave me the confidence I needed to accept jobs that took me throughout the Midwest on my own.

When I went through my major heartbreak with Tom, you were the one whose shoulder I cried on. You were the one I trusted. You helped me get through it.

Dad, your alcoholism has been a part of our lives for a very long time. We didn't get here overnight. It is running your life. When I call home to check in, if it is too late in the evening, you're drunk. You get on the phone and your speech is slurred. When we talk later in the week you don't even remember our conversations. Sometimes you're passed out, and we don't get to talk at all.

When I come to visit you, and I'm on my way out to walk the

dog, if you're in the garage I'll try to wait a little while because I don't want to catch you secretly pouring a drink. I do this to save you embarrassment. Or else I try to make a lot of noise in the laundry room so you know I'm coming, and you can hide the alcohol.

If I show up at your house late in the evening, you're drunk. I see it in your eyes, hear it in your speech, and watch you move back and forth from the kitchen cupboard to the couch, with an occasional trip to the garage to drink from your hidden supply.

I love you, and I don't like seeing alcoholism sucking the life out of you. We're all here together because we want you to accept help. We're here to help. Will you accept our help today?

Love,

Your daughter, Tina

A wife wrote the next letter to her husband:

Dear Geoff,

You know that I love you. I have loved you since the day we met. How many times have I told you the story of how I knew when I first saw you that you and I were going to be together forever? I still love you that much today. I love how you are with our children. I love all the things you do for us, and the way you take care of so many things for us. You are consistently taking care of all of us, even my mother. I respect how well you do your job, and how respected you are by those you work with. I admire how dedicated you are toward your family and your profession. I also love your knowledge of so many things, and how willing you are to share your knowledge with the people who ask. You are a wonderful father and have been a wonderful husband. I cherish you to the highest degree.

Now, though, I see you fighting the demons at night. Your alcoholism has caused so many things to change in our lives. Because of the alcohol, the trust I have in you has diminished terribly. I fear for the safety of the children when you are alone and in charge of them. I live in constant fear that you will drink and drive the children around in the car. Then, three weeks ago, my worst nightmare came true. You drove Toni to a party, and you were drunk. This is the only time I can prove you've driven one of our children while you were drinking, but I know in my heart—and so do you—that this is not the only time you have done this. You also lose your patience easily with the little ones when you have been drinking at night, and as much as they love you, I see the fear and confusion in their eyes when you have been drinking.

Your behavior changes so radically when you have been drinking. You lose focus, and all of the wonderful things you set out to accomplish just fall by the wayside. Each summer for the past four years has ended in sadness and waste. You start out with so many wonderful plans, and then by the end of the summer, you have been drunk so many of the days that very little has been accomplished. The things you have finished have only been done halfway.

I also see that you are likely to do the opposite of what I would personally like you to do when you've been drinking. If I say it's time to put the kids to bed, you disregard what I say and allow them to stay up another hour. The alcohol has caused problems between you and me, and our marriage is suffering.

This letter brings me to what I want for you, and for me and for our family. Geoff, your alcoholism has caused us problems. I love you and want to work with you to make a commitment to seeing you get help—and becoming you again. I cannot tell you how much I love you. I know we can, together, make all of this better. We have work to do. *You* have work to do. I do not blame you for this, but I need you to work with me and with the kids to make a future for us together. Please tell me today that we will have a chance at the future, because you are going to go today and commit to a new life. Please accept the help I am offering you today.

Love,

Your wife, Julianna

An adult granddaughter wrote the third letter to her grand-mother.

> Dear Granny,
>
> You and I have always had a special bond. We like to sit and talk about life and philosophy, and it always seems we end up solving the problems of the world. I can always count on you for anything and everything. I think you know you are like a second mother to me. I told you just the other day how much Christmastime means to me, and I thank you for providing me with so many warm memories. As far back as I can remember, every stay at your house was a joy for me. I know you always go out of your way to make things special for me.
>
> I love you so much—it's more than love, even—you're just more important to me than you could possibly imagine. You and Granddad keep this family together; you make us whole. I am here for you today, because I want you to be healthy. While I may speak of the past, this is about the here and now—today, and our future together as a family. So please know this is not meant to hurt you, but about bringing our family together with love.
>
> Granny, when you are sober, you are as reliable as a clock. Since there are long periods when you do not drink, I can let myself ignore the fact that you suffer from this disease and just concentrate on the good times. I always think, "Maybe she won't drink again. Maybe that last time was her last."
>
> Last spring, when a binge landed you in the hospital, Mom, Dad, Janie, and I decided for about the third time that we were going to do *something* to get you help. But then you got pneumonia, and that allowed me to forget about the drinking and concentrate on other things. It is easy for me to pretend nothing is wrong—especially a week or so after a drinking binge. It is more comfortable for me to concentrate on the good stuff.
>
> Last April, after I got back from visiting you and Granddad, my mom told me you drank again. I was so surprised and all

those old feelings I push out of my mind came rushing back. They always come back when I hear about a binge. Questions run through my mind. "What made her do it this time?" "How bad was it?" "How long did it last?" "How far and where did she drive?" "Did she hurt herself?" "Is she at home or in the hospital?" "Is Granddad okay?"

You may not know this, but I usually find out when you've gone on a binge, even a small one. Mom might say, "We think Granny's drinking." It isn't a secret. Everyone knows, everyone hurts; it's on everyone's mind.

The Thursday you started drinking this last time, I remember coming home and finding you sitting in the kitchen. Granddad was doing the dishes, and you and I had a great conversation for about five minutes before I realized your laugh was a little too hearty, you were talking a little too much. The realization came upon me like a slap in the face. I actually backed away from you physically and could only respond in one-word sentences. I just wanted to get out of there and forget what I was seeing. When Mom told me you had drank, it felt like a punch in the stomach.

I don't have many memories of witnessing your binges. Instead, what I have is a feeling that is always with me. It is a fear that nags at me, "Someday Granny is going to die of alcoholism." A lot of the time, I rely on my denial so I can go on without going crazy from that thought. A picture that stays in my head is you lying dead in a snowdrift, having passed out after a binge. I read about a woman in her 40s dying that way a few years ago. The image stays with me. Granny, I don't want to have those kinds of thoughts about you.

A few days ago, I started thinking about the fact that despite this devastating, debilitating disease you've been suffering with for nearly half a century, you've accomplished so much and deserve the love and respect of so many. You're really quite amazing. It takes a strong woman to do what you have done for so long in the face of a disease that kills so many. I know you can beat this disease, but that is not accomplished alone. If it could be done alone, you would have done it by now. But no one recovers alone. It requires reaching out to others.

So will you please accept the help we are offering? The help I am asking you to take? We are together as a family, and I promise I will do my part. Please take the first step toward recovery with us today.

Love,
 Miranda

Your Bottom Line

When an intervention is well planned, about 85 percent of people being asked to accept help do. But that leaves 15 percent who refuse to accept help and choose to continue drinking or using other drugs. If this happens, we present our bottom lines to the alcoholic. Bottom lines are those things we will no longer do to support the disease of addiction. They include the ways we are going to take care of ourselves.

You already are prepared to set your bottom line if you did two things earlier in the book: (1) identified ways you've enabled the alcoholic in the past; and (2) identified any leverage you may have. If you haven't yet done these things, turn back to section 2. The decision to discontinue an enabling behavior is a bottom line.

If you go to the Tools section of this book, you will find examples of bottom lines. Use these examples to help you brainstorm. Once you know what your bottom line is, write it on a piece of paper separate from the letter to the alcoholic. It might read something like this: "Barbara, you may not realize how much pain your addiction to prescription pills and alcohol has caused me. I've learned that I've been doing things—thinking I was helping you—which all along were only helping the addiction. I love you too much to continue doing that. Today, I have made a commitment to only support your recovery. For this reason, if you do not accept help for your drug problem, you cannot live in my house anymore. You will have to find your own apartment. My kids—your nieces—love you, but lately they've told me you frighten them. I must protect them from the addiction, so until you get help, you cannot spend time with the children. Please accept the help we're offering you today."

You can hear how much love is expressed even as the bottom line is being delivered. We aren't trying to blame or shame the alcoholic. This is not the tone we want to set in our bottom lines. We use *love first* in our message. We make it clear that our actions are based on our intention to support recovery and to stop supporting addiction. We also make it clear that we will no longer let the addiction take priority over the welfare of our families.

Bottom lines cause negative consequences to fall upon the addict *only if she makes a choice to choose alcohol and drugs over sobriety and recovery*. We aren't doing these things *to* her. Do you see the difference here? We are only saying what we will and will not support, and how we'll carry that out in a practical manner. The alcoholic makes the choice for herself.

Quite often, a resistant addict changes her mind once she hears the team's bottom lines. She sees her life crumbling before her and going to treatment becomes a better option. You've probably heard people say it's no good if she goes to treatment against her will. Well, she's not going against her will. She is making a choice based on information she is given during the intervention. She can say "yes" or she can say "no."

The Hazelden Foundation did a twenty-five-year study comparing the success rates between people who came into treatment on their own and people who were ordered into treatment by the courts. The success rates were virtually the same for both groups. All alcoholics and addicts in treatment struggle with denial and anger. The treatment process helps them to work through these challenges. The way an addict gets into treatment is not as much of a factor as what happens while she's in treatment.

In some states, you can petition the courts to order an addicted person into treatment. In Florida, for example, the Marchman Act allows family members or friends to go to court and ask that an alcoholic or addict be mandated into treatment. Most states allow parents to court order children under eighteen years of age into treatment. This can be very effective if the addicted person is so sick or rebellious you have no other way of helping her.

We worked with a family intervening on their fifteen-year-old daughter. She was addicted to street drugs and had an older boyfriend, a drug dealer, who had more influence over her than her parents. The family decided to get a court order, but not mention it unless their daughter refused help. They hoped their influence would carry the intervention, and they wouldn't have to use the court order. But that didn't happen. In the end, the daughter refused to accept treatment and her father had to use the court order as a bottom line. He said something like this: "We'd hoped you would come to this decision on your own. But we also prepared ourselves for the chance that you would not. We are your parents, and your welfare is our responsibility. For that reason, we have obtained a court order stipulating that you go to treatment. Either you go with us now, or the police will pick you up and escort you there." The girl cried, but she agreed to go with her parents.

Remember, you only share your bottom line with the alcoholic *if* he chooses to continue in addiction and refuse recovery. Don't ever use a bottom line as a bluff. If you say it, you need to be 100 percent sure you'll follow through. If you don't follow through, you'll empower the disease. The addict now knows you don't mean what you say, and the intervention is reduced to an exercise in futility. Test yourself sufficiently before choosing your bottom line. If a voice says, "I'll never do this," find another bottom line.

If you have leverage, but don't want to use it, explore your reasons behind that decision. If you're afraid the addict will be angry with you, maybe you need to tell yourself that it's all right for him to get angry. Some people put it in perspective by saying to themselves, "I'd rather have him angry with me than dead. I'll take anger over that any day."

Put the focus on yourself. Make decisions based on what you know is ultimately right. Don't worry about the addict's reaction. Maybe he needs to go through anger before he can reach a place of change. We've heard many recovering alcoholics say, "The person I was most angry with then, I am most grateful to today."

One last thought. Always end your bottom line statement by repeating the question with which you ended your letter—"Will you accept the help we're offering you today?" Give the alcoholic a chance to change his mind. Watch the tone of your voice when you are reading your bottom line. If you're seething with anger, even the most loving words can feel like bullets. Stay in a place of love. If the alcoholic says no to treatment, remember, it is the stranglehold of his disease that prevents him from reaching out for help.

SECTION

4

The Intervention

Listing Possible Objections
and Your Answers

When intervening on someone with an alcohol or other drug problem, you are undoing all of the addict's hard work to safeguard the addiction from outside interference. As soon as the intervention begins, the alcoholic realizes that the power has shifted to the group, and his old methods of manipulation and avoidance are no longer going to work. His mind races as he looks for an escape route. When he's found one, he'll present it to you in the form of an objection. It's the team's job not to let the alcoholic slip through. This can't be done impromptu during the intervention. You must plan ahead.

Objections don't indicate a pending upset. When the alcoholic verbalizes an objection, she is giving you an opportunity to demonstrate how thoroughly prepared you are. When you tell her the team has already addressed that problem, your seriousness becomes unmistakable. With no escape routes, the alcoholic usually will accept help.

Prepare for the alcoholic's objections. Involve the entire team. If you need help getting started, turn to the Tools section. Have the team brainstorm all the possible objections the alcoholic may raise. The detail person should list them.

Next, decide how to answer each objection, and determine what action steps you need to take. For instance, if you anticipate Cousin Vinnie's wedding as a possible objection, go to Vinnie and ask him to write a letter. The letter might say something like: "I thought you might refuse the help you need because of my wedding, but the best wedding present you could give me is going into treatment today. I'd never want to think my wedding was the reason you didn't get help." Read this letter only if the objection comes up. If the alcoholic doesn't mention Vinnie's wedding, don't make a point of reminding him.

Of course, if the alcoholic happens to be Vinnie's best man, handling the objection is more complicated. It may be wise to wait until after the wedding. If it's too dangerous to delay, go ahead and intervene before the wedding. Ask Vinnie to participate. He can give the alcoholic permission to miss the wedding by explaining that his life is more important than being best man.

Some objections are harder to answer than others because they are based on opinion rather than fact. Vinnie's wedding is a fact, as is Vinnie's response that he wants the alcoholic to go to treatment. Facts are difficult to debate. Opinions, however, are a different matter. Let's imagine that the alcoholic says, "I'm not going to treatment, because I don't think I have a problem." In this case, he's using opinion to object to treatment. If the team attempts to change his opinion, they could start a power struggle the alcoholic will most likely win. If the alcoholic's objections are based on opinions, don't try to change his thinking. That hasn't worked in the past, and it won't work during an intervention.

So how do we handle objections based on opinion? First keep the focus on the group, rather than on the alcoholic. Speak from the group's position, not to the alcoholic's point of view. Let's see how this works using the example from above: "I'm not going to treatment, because I don't think I have a problem." The chairperson avoids getting into a debate with the alcoholic by saying: "We've learned that people with alcohol problems are the last to know they have a problem. I think you'd agree with me when I say that none of us would choose to do this unless we truly believed alcohol is causing problems in your life. We're not asking you to determine if you have a problem. We're asking you to get a professional assessment. If you don't have a problem, they'll tell you. We've taken care of setting up the appointment. We're just asking you to find out from a professional."

Nothing the chairperson says opens the door to a power struggle between the alcoholic and the team. The alcoholic may still refuse treatment, but the integrity of the intervention is not damaged. This is important because a properly executed intervention has immense impact upon an alcoholic even if he doesn't accept help, and it increases the likelihood that he will change his mind and accept help at a later date.

Let's look at another objection, one that appears to be based on fact but is really a thinly veiled opinion: "How can you say I have a problem? You've been out drinking with me plenty. At that Super Bowl party, you put away your share of beer." The alcoholic is observing some facts about a team member's drinking, but the unstated opinion is, "No one who drinks alcohol can tell me I have a problem."

While no one with an alcohol or other drug problem should be on the intervention team, we don't demand that all team members be teetotalers. By challenging someone else's drinking habits, the alcoholic is attempting to shift the focus off herself and onto someone else. If she succeeds, she'll grab the power away from the group and the intervention will fold into chaos. To deal successfully with this objection, avoid becoming defensive. Don't say, "Hey, Bob might have a few drinks, but he's never had a problem with alcohol." You are now reacting to the alcoholic by countering her opinion with your opinion, and you put her in control of what is happening in the intervention. Keep the focus on the alcoholic's problem and needs. The chairperson can respond, "Today we're talking about your drinking. We've learned that it's not about how much you drink but what happens to you when you drink."

If objections are based on personal responsibilities—money, work, kids, or pets—offer good solutions. For instance, if the alcoholic says, "I can't go to treatment because I have to take care

of Rover," the chairperson says, "We thought of that. You know
how well Rover and Jack's dog get along, so Jack is taking care of
Rover for you." Or if the alcoholic says, "I can't afford to take
time off work for treatment; I have a mortgage to pay," the chairperson says, "We thought of that. We've all chipped in to cover
any cash shortage you might have so you can go to treatment
and pay your bills this month. You can pay us back when you're
on your feet again." If the addict says, "I can't leave my house
that long," the chairperson says, "We thought of that. Sean will
pick up your mail each day after work. Pat will mow your lawn,
and Kay's going to stop by to water your plants."

Answering objections based on work-related responsibilities is
such a critical issue that we've devoted an entire section to the
topic. We suggest you turn back to "Involving the Workplace," in
section 3, for a review. Objections regarding work may give an alcoholic the best possible escape route.

Sometimes an alcoholic will hang strong to an objection. No
matter how well prepared your answer is, he won't change his
mind. One objection alcoholics tend to cling to is this: "Okay, I
may drink too much, but I can stop on my own and that's what
I'm going to do." The chairperson may say, "Doctors do not recommend that people quit drinking on their own. Quitting cold
turkey from alcohol can be dangerous. It can cause seizures or
worse. Also, we've learned that long-term success requires the
right kind of help. It's not the quitting you need help with.
You've done that before. It's staying quit and being content
sober." When the alcoholic remains steadfast to the idea of quitting on his own, the chairperson can say, "While we don't agree
that this is the best way to handle the problem, it is your decision. However, if your way doesn't work and you take another
drink, we ask you to promise us that you'll then do it our way
and go to treatment. Is that a deal?" Most alcoholics will agree.

If an alcoholic or addict insists on quitting on his own, specify
that quitting means abstaining from all addictive drugs, including

alcohol. Quitting alcohol doesn't mean switching to marijuana, and quitting cocaine doesn't mean switching to beer. The chairperson can say, "We've learned that using other mood-altering drugs such as marijuana is called switched addiction. We ask that you don't switch to other mood-altering drugs once you've quit."

All objections are answered by the chairperson. A single, consistent voice keeps order to an intervention, whereas several people talking to the alcoholic creates the impression of a free-for-all. When responding to objections, be brief. If an objection can be answered in one sentence, all the better.

Since the chairperson is designated to reply to all objections, he or she should role-play with a team member acting as the alcoholic. The team member reads each objection the team has listed, and the chairperson gives the answers. Practice answering the objections with the chairperson until he or she feels confident. To make things comfortable and natural, the chairperson shouldn't memorize answers but rather put them in his or her own words.

One last thought about objections. As important as it is to be prepared for them, the alcoholic or addict rarely brings up many—if any—objections. While we want you to be ready for any possibility, we don't want to give the impression that you'll be facing a barrage of objections during the intervention. It is more likely that the alcoholic will not object at all. Rarely do we hear two or more objections during an intervention.

Rehearsing the Intervention

A rehearsal is necessary before the actual intervention. Everyone who plans to participate in the intervention should attend. If a team member cannot physically attend the rehearsal, ask her to participate over a speaker phone. Or she could meet with you before the intervention to review the details of the rehearsal. No one goes into an intervention without knowing exactly what to do.

Go over the checklist with the detail person for the last time and make sure all tasks are complete. Call the treatment center and confirm your appointment. Be sure all financial arrangements are in place. You don't want anything to go wrong when the alcoholic arrives at the treatment center.

There are four phases to rehearsing the intervention. The first phase is to edit and rehearse the letters. Each person reads his or her letter aloud while the group listens carefully to both tone and content. There are six considerations when editing letters:

1. *Remove negative content.* Anger, blame, or judgment can creep into letters without our awareness. Families and friends of alcoholics and addicts may feel angry about the addiction. Sometimes anger shows up in the words we use or in the way we read the letter. If your teammates hear something in your letter that sounds angry, remove it or find another way to say it.

2. *Listen for a message of love and concern.* Does the letter communicate empathy and support? Approaching the

alcoholic with love first may be the most powerful force for breaking down denial while preserving the alcoholic's dignity.

3. *Use firsthand experiences when talking about the addiction and refrain from repeating secondhand information.* Hearsay sounds like gossip and can trigger a defensive reaction from the alcoholic. There are rare exceptions to this rule. One example of using hearsay appropriately is when a team member lives far away and hasn't witnessed the addiction firsthand. That person might then say, "You and I haven't seen each other in the last few years, so I haven't seen this problem firsthand. But Mom has confided in me about her concerns regarding your cocaine use, which has caused me to worry as well."

4. *Is the letter written in first person, using the word* I *rather than* we? All intervention letters are to be written in the first person. When you write your letter speak for yourself, not for the group. Saying "I love you" is more intimate and emotionally powerful than saying, "We love you." If a letter isn't written in first person, rewrite it by replacing the word *we* with the word *I*.

5. *End the letter by asking the alcoholic to accept help.* Each letter must end with a clear and direct appeal for the alcoholic or addict to accept help. If you don't ask the alcoholic to accept help, she's not going to know what you want from her. Make sure each letter ends with something like, "Will you go into treatment today and accept the help we are offering you?"

6. *Have all team members completed letters?* Work together to help team members who are having difficulty completing their letters. If someone can't decide what to write, suggest he listen to other people's letters. This will help him come up with ideas of his own. Schedule twenty minutes for people to rewrite or finish letters.

The second phase of the rehearsal is to determine the order in which the letters will be read. The sequence in which you read your letters can strengthen your intervention. The alcoholic will make his decision about treatment after he listens to all the letters. For this reason, the last letter may be the most important. So ask yourselves who the alcoholic will have the most difficulty saying no to. Have that person read his or her letter last. For instance, if the alcoholic is angry with his wife and she reads her letter last, he may find it easy to say no to her and refuse treatment. However, if the grandmother he adores reads her letter last, he's more likely to accept help.

Now identify a person who commands the alcoholic's respect. This person should read his letter first. The alcoholic won't easily walk out of the intervention while someone he respects is reading a letter to him. Once the alcoholic listens to the first letter, it is highly unlikely he'll get up and leave the intervention.

A person who has a strained relationship with the alcoholic should read her letter between two people with strong emotional influences over the alcoholic. For instance, if the alcoholic is angry with his wife, but has a good relationship with his mother and uncle, have the wife read her letter between the two. The uncle and mother serve as buffers for angry reactions the alcoholic may have toward his wife.

The order in which you choose to read may also be decided after listening to the content of the letters. A person may have a close emotional bond with the alcoholic, yet write a letter that is more intellectual than emotional. This may not be the best letter to read last, but perhaps a good letter to read first or second. Do whatever feels right in the context of your family and sounds right to your ear.

The third phase is to choose your seating arrangement. Sitting at a table creates a barrier between people, so avoid the kitchen table and use the living room. Arrange the furniture slightly so everyone is turned toward the alcoholic. Seat the alcoholic on a couch between two people he loves and respects. Seat the chairperson between the alcoholic and the door, so if the alcoholic decides to leave, the chairperson can follow him outside and ask him to return. If anyone has a troubled relationship with the alcoholic, keep some space between the two of them. Think about who you will seat directly across from the alcoholic. That person will have direct eye contact with the alcoholic throughout the intervention.

The fourth phase of rehearsing the intervention is to do everything exactly as you expect to do it the day of the intervention. This means no smoking, eating, joking, or talking. No one gets up until the rehearsal is over. Turn off telephone ringers, cell phones, and pagers. Put the dog outside. Think of all possible distractions and interruptions, and eliminate them.

Now begin. Everyone takes their seats. The chairperson leads off by going to the door and greeting the alcoholic. Another team member can play the alcoholic if this is helpful. Everyone reads their letters. The chairperson rehearses what he'll say if the alcoholic accepts help, and what he'll say if he doesn't. Everyone rehearses their bottom lines in case the alcoholic refuses help. After the bottom lines are read, the chairperson asks again if the alcoholic will accept help. When you've finished the rehearsal, decide if you need to go through it a second time.

Set aside some time to rehearse the objections and answers. One person can play the alcoholic and read the objections to the chairperson. Go over the objections until the chairperson feels comfortable with his or her answers.

You may find that reading your letter is a very emotional experience. If you become overwhelmed, stop and take a few deep breaths. Once you feel composed, start reading again. Most people find that once they've read the letter at the rehearsal, they aren't as emotionally overwhelmed during the intervention.

If the location for the rehearsal is not the same as the location for the intervention, make a diagram of the room you plan to use and create a seating chart. Then rehearse the intervention as if you are at the other location. If you're using the alcoholic's house for the intervention, you might say, "Okay, we're going to meet at the gas station two blocks from Anita's house at 9:15 A.M. We'll drive to her house together, park, and walk to the front door as a group. Tom will answer the door. We'll all take our seats in the living room while the chairperson goes into the kitchen to greet Anita." Once you've set the scenario, begin your rehearsal.

Feelings of anxiety are normal when planning an intervention. The closer you get to the event, the greater the anxiety. Most people report that they don't sleep well the night before an intervention. Talking about your fears can help. It also helps to plan some fun at the rehearsal. Put together a buffet of sandwiches, snacks, desserts, and nonalcoholic beverages. Eating and socializing helps everyone relax.

Some Thoughts for Intervention Day

It's the day of the intervention, and if you're like most people, your pulse is racing and your stomach is full of butterflies. The anticipation period before the intervention is more stressful than the intervention itself. Once the intervention begins and the letters are being read, your anxiety level will drop significantly.

While watching the *Oprah Winfrey Show* on television one day, we heard Oprah mention that she had participated in an intervention. She described it as one of the most loving things she had ever experienced. We think you'll probably have a similar reaction after your intervention. Intervention gives you an opportunity to be an instrument of love.

When going into the intervention, renew your resolve to stick with your plan and trust the process. If this is the first time you've participated in an intervention, you have no previous experience to prepare you for what to expect. You may feel as if you are jumping into an abyss with no idea where you will land. Just remember, many people have successfully taken this road before you. Even though you've never done it before, intervention is a tried and true way of helping someone with an alcohol or other drug problem.

Keep your focus on yourself, your team, and your plan. Don't start reacting to what the alcoholic does during the intervention. If you focus on the alcoholic rather than your plan, the intervention process will dissolve into unmanageability. If the alcoholic isn't responding as you expected, all the more reason to stick to your plan. Have faith and keep moving forward even if all appears lost. As Dr. Robert Schuller, author and pastor, reminds us: "What appears to be an end of the road may simply be a bend in the road." In many ways, intervention is an act of faith.

If the alcoholic refuses treatment, read your bottom lines. Remember, your bottom line is a way of saying, "I will not support this disease." It is a way to take care of yourself when addiction continues to attack your family. You are not punishing the alcoholic or addict. The alcoholic brings the consequences upon himself by choosing addiction over recovery. He can avoid consequences in one of two ways: (1) choosing recovery or (2) convincing people to enable his addiction again. If people stop supporting the addiction, the alcoholic who refuses treatment is likely to choose recovery in the weeks or months following the intervention.

Once you present your bottom line to the alcoholic, don't change your mind later on. If you do, you are empowering the disease. You are, in essence, telling the alcoholic: "I said I wouldn't support your disease anymore, but I can't follow through. It's easier to go along with the addiction."

Once all letters are read, give the addict a chance to talk. Sometimes a refusal turns into an agreement when the alcoholic can talk through her fears and frustrations. Although the chairperson is designated to answer objections during the intervention, be flexible when the alcoholic is speaking to the group. The right words from another team member may be very helpful.

If the alcoholic agrees to accept help, tell her how proud you are of her. Everyone should get up from their seats and give her a hug. This gets everyone on their feet and ready to go. The chairperson can move things forward by saying something like: "We have a suitcase packed for you, and it's already in the trunk. Your dad and I are driving you to the treatment center, and everyone else will follow in a separate car. We have an 11:30 appointment, so we should get going if we want to get there on time." Then, lead the alcoholic outside and into the car. In most cases, the alcoholic will leave immediately or right after a quick bathroom stop.

Take care of details so the alcoholic doesn't have to make phone calls, stop to buy cigarettes, or tie up loose ends. If you anticipate that the alcoholic will say she needs to make some phone calls before leaving, have a cellular phone ready for her to use in the car. Sometimes an alcoholic will agree to treatment but demand to take a shower first. If this happens, ask her to take a ten-minute shower so you can still make the appointment on time.

If the treatment center is out of state and you have time to kill before the departure of the airplane, drive to the airport and have lunch together. Celebrate. Keep the conversation light and have a good time. Levity and laughter will do the alcoholic more good than a serious conversation about her problems. If the alcoholic wants to drink on the plane, let her. Many an alcoholic describes her last binge as the one she had on the way to treatment.

The honesty and love of intervention bring families back together where the dishonesty and anger of addiction had ripped them apart. Intervention opens the doors of communication and is a springboard for change. It is the most powerful tool for families who want to help an addicted loved one. No matter what the alcoholic decides, you always will know you did the very best you could to help her.

Notes for the Chairperson

As chairperson, you set the tone for the entire team during the intervention. This is a job for your most positive emotions. If you stay calm and avoid anger, the team will follow your lead. Remember: *intervention is an act of love.* This will help you stay on track, remain calm, and preserve the dignity of the addicted person.

As chairperson, you'll play the roles of host, guide, and spokesperson. You'll greet the alcoholic, seat him, and make the opening statement. You cue the team members to begin reading letters, you answer objections, and ask the alcoholic to accept help. If the alcoholic refuses help, you introduce the bottom lines. Once the team members read the bottom lines, you again ask the alcoholic to accept help.

Review the sample intervention at the end of this section. Pay close attention to what the chairperson says. You'll notice that he remains calm, speaks clearly, and uses as few words as possible. When the alcoholic speaks, he listens and doesn't interrupt.

At the rehearsal, practice your greeting as well as opening and closing statements. Use the following examples to help you decide what you might say during the intervention:

Greeting: Kathy, everybody is here today because we love you very much and have some important things to share with you. Come on in and take a seat right over here.

Opening: Everyone has taken time to write you a letter.

We'd like you to listen as we read our letters to you. Your grandmother would like to begin.

Closing #1: Kathy, we've taken care of everything for you. You don't have to worry about anything. Will you accept the help we're offering you today? *(agrees to treatment)* I know I can speak for the entire group when I say we're very proud of you. *(everyone gets up and gives hugs)*

Closing #2: (when treatment is refused) Kathy, we've made some personal decisions in case you decided not to get help. We love you too much to continue doing anything that will support your addiction, and we've decided to take care of ourselves because your addiction causes us pain, too. We'd like to share the decisions we've made with you. Your grandmother will begin. *(everyone reads bottom lines)* Kathy, will you accept the help we're offering you today? *(still refuses help)* Getting treatment is ultimately your decision. If you change your mind, you can call any one of us for help. If you choose to stay in your addiction, we must stand by the decisions we have just shared with you.

If you feel more confident reading your remarks rather than speaking extemporaneously, go ahead and write them down on a separate piece of paper. We've worked with several chairpersons who read their closing statements without diminishing the effectiveness of the intervention.

If the alcoholic refuses help, you can ask him why. This gives the alcoholic an opportunity to express his thoughts and feelings. By listening carefully, you may discover the reason behind his resistance. For instance, when asked, an alcoholic told his family he wouldn't go to treatment because, "No one is going to lock me up in a nut house." He thought he was being committed to a lock-down ward in a psychiatric hospital. The chairman immediately pulled out a color brochure of the alcohol and drug treatment center. He showed the alcoholic pictures of the nicely decorated rooms and the beautiful campus. He assured the alcoholic that no one was planning to lock him up and explained that staying in treatment would be his choice. With his fears alleviated, the alcoholic agreed to go.

Sometimes the alcoholic's reasons for not accepting help keep changing, and he won't accept any solutions. In these cases, the real reason he won't go is because he wants to drink. Every so often, letting alcoholics have a drink before leaving for treatment gives them the relief and fortitude to accept help.

If you don't know how to respond to something the alcoholic says, pause and give yourself time to think. Rely on two considerations: (1) speak to the alcoholic from a place of love and (2) stay focused on the goal of treatment. We suggest memorizing a standard answer you can use as a safety net if you find yourself at a loss for words. The standard answer we use is: "I hear what you are saying, but today we're talking about how we're going to help you with your (alcohol or drug) problem."

This simple statement is a powerful workhorse during an intervention. It assures the alcoholic that you are listening to what he is saying while bringing the focus back to treatment. If the alcoholic tries to pull you into an argument, you can repeat the standard answer over again, regardless of what the alcoholic says to you. When you do this, you keep the focus on your message and avoid being pulled off track. Repeating the standard answer is an excellent technique for deflating an alcoholic's long-winded debate designed to deflect focus off himself and onto other issues.

Sometimes an objection comes up that must be answered by someone other than the chairperson. This happened during an intervention we facilitated on a middle-aged, divorced alcoholic. At one point the alcoholic turned to his grown children and said, "This isn't about my drinking. This is about your anger toward me because I divorced your mother." The chairperson knew he couldn't speak for the kids in this instance. The son responded to his dad by saying, "I do have feelings about the divorce. But my concerns about your drinking started before your divorce. The only reason we're here today is because we love you and want you to get help." His answer was a version of the standard answer. First he assured his father that he was listening to him, and then he brought the focus back to getting help for the alcohol problem. It's a good idea for everyone on the team to memorize the standard answer in case they have to respond to an unexpected objection.

Once the intervention begins, trust the process. If the alcoholic refuses help, keep your team focused on the bottom lines. You've put a process into motion and, by staying your course, you have a good chance of seeing change happen.

Making Team Decisions

Intervention is not the end of the story. It's the beginning. Prepare yourself for the journey ahead. It won't always be easy. Whether the alcoholic goes into treatment or not, he will test you. He'll be difficult and unpredictable, and it won't be easy on anyone around him. The addiction and all the related problems didn't happen overnight, and they won't be solved overnight.

If, after the intervention, you find yourself thinking, "I can handle this on my own now," you're in a vulnerable position. Believing you don't need the help of others makes you more susceptible to the alcoholic's manipulations. Addiction can skillfully trick people into enabling the disease and short-circuiting the treatment process. Alcoholics can always manipulate one person more easily than a group of people. So once the intervention is over, use the power of the group. Foster an *interdependent* relationship with your team members—a shared dependence and mutual support of one another. You need support now more than ever.

Be prepared for your addicted loved one to attempt to persuade you to support his disease again. He may call and tell you he's leaving treatment early. He'll ask you to pick him up. He'll convince you he doesn't need treatment anymore. We've seen many people intervene on loved ones only to turn around and "rescue" them from treatment a few days later. If you find yourself ready to do something like this, call your team members and talk it out before you take action. If the alcoholic starts asking you to do favors for him, say, "I'll have to get back to you on that." Then call your team members and, when possible, the addictions counselor. Don't decide alone. Make team decisions.

Intervention puts the wheels of change into motion, and change doesn't often come quietly. It may shake up your life. You learned certain survival skills that helped you cope with the addiction in your family. These changes in your behaviors happened gradually and subconsciously. Your focus was on the alcoholic or addict's behaviors, not on how the problem was changing you. When a family supports recovery, it also must begin its own personal recovery program. This helps family members identify how the addiction has changed them, and how to begin healing themselves and their relationships. A passage from Al-Anon's *Courage to Change* expresses this well: "One of the effects of alcoholism is that many of us have devalued our talents, feelings, achievements, and desires. In Al-Anon we learn to know, appreciate, and express our true selves."

Begin by attending the treatment center's family program. Continue your recovery in Al-Anon, Nar-Anon, or Families Anonymous. These Twelve Step groups are the best way for family members of alcoholics and addicts to embrace recovery and positive change.

Intervening on an Adolescent

No amount of alcohol or other drugs is safe for a child or adolescent. Addiction progresses more quickly in young people than it does in adults. A study by the National Institute on Alcohol Abuse and Alcoholism shows more than 40 percent of people who begin drinking before the age of fifteen become alcoholic. More than 24 percent who begin drinking at age seventeen become alcoholic. When young people wait until age twenty-one or twenty-two to drink alcohol, their risk of alcoholism drops to 10 percent.

In adolescence, we go through more physical and emotional changes in a shorter amount of time than any other period in our lives. Mood-altering substances block the development of social skills and emotional maturity. A sixteen-year-old who's been drinking for five years has the maturity of an eleven-year-old. Our children are bombarded with messages about the pleasures and benefits of drinking alcohol when they watch television and look at magazines. Yet we expect them not to drink. In her book *Deadly Persuasion*, Jean Kilbourne writes, "One of the most striking examples of advertising is the very successful and long-running campaign for Absolut Vodka. . . . Collecting Absolut ads is now a common pastime for elementary-school children, who swap them like baseball cards." She goes on to say, "What's the best way to appeal to young people? One way, of course, is to present the product as strictly for adults—as in the so-called moderation messages of the alcohol and tobacco industries. . . . Another ploy is to use cute little animals and cartoon characters like Spuds MacKenzie and the Budweiser frogs, lizards, and Dalmatians." Although alcohol presents the number one drug problem among youth, illegal drugs are easy to obtain in our communities. Children can frequently purchase them from fellow students in the corridors and classrooms of schools.

Marijuana use is tolerated as a relatively benign drug by some people. Some young people believe marijuana is nonaddictive and doesn't cause serious problems for the user. The reality of marijuana use is more disturbing. Some of the consequences are:

- impaired judgment
- high-risk behaviors
- addiction
- unknown additives (PCP, herbicides)
- short-term memory loss
- car accidents
- reduced learning capacity
- acute anxiety and paranoia
- lost potential and low motivation
- increased risk of cancer
- increased risk for sexual activity, pregnancy, HIV infection
- decreased testosterone levels affecting developing bodies

Young people can successfully hide their use of alcohol or other drugs from their parents for years. Parents often ignore the symptoms of drug use or dismiss them as normal adolescent behavior. But experiencing serious and repeated problems isn't a normal part of growing up. If you suspect an adolescent has an alcohol or other drug problem but are not sure, take the quiz "Is Our Teen Chemically Dependent?" in the Tools section and review the symptoms of abuse and addiction. If your child is experiencing some of these problems, consult with a counselor at an adolescent treatment facility.

When intervening on an adolescent, avoid acting like an authority figure. Don't preach, lecture, or use your intervention letter to express your disappointment in the child. Approach your child with respect and talk about the addiction as a disease. At the same time, don't try to pass yourself off as your kid's best pal either. Be a parent first. Your child needs loving but firm guidance.

Refer to the addiction as a family problem and express your commitment to participate in the treatment process. Inform your child that everyone plans to attend the family education program and counseling sessions. Make a commitment to attend Al-Anon, Nar-Anon, or Families Anonymous meetings weekly. Your example will influence how your child does in treatment and recovery.

If you are concerned that your child will refuse to go into treatment or try to run away, consider obtaining a court order. Most states allow parents to use the court system to order children under eighteen years of age into a chemical dependency treatment center. If you obtain a court order, use it as your bottom line. Proceed with the intervention without mentioning the court order. Give your child the dignity to accept help on his or her own. If he or she refuses help, use your bottom line to inform your child of the court order. We've worked with parents who've explained it like this: "It was my hope that you would choose help on your own. As your parent, it is my job to help you when you are unable or unwilling to help yourself. For that reason, I have obtained a court order that mandates you into treatment. You have the choice to go to treatment on your own, but if you refuse, the police will escort you to the treatment center today."

If either parent abuses alcohol, prescription drugs, or illegal drugs, your child may ask you to answer for this behavior. You'll have to be honest with yourself about your own chemical use. If alcohol is a prerequisite for a good time, is your usual way to reduce stress, or is part of your nightly ritual, you may have to reconsider your relationship with alcohol and the message you're sending to your child. If the adolescent brings up your alcohol use during the intervention, you can say something like, "Today we're talking about *your* alcohol and marijuana problem. But I promise to be honest about my alcohol use when I talk with the treatment staff and make any changes they recommend." If you say that, however, you'd better follow through.

When looking for an adolescent treatment center, be sure it has a strong family component and uses the Twelve Step model of recovery. Look for a program that involves the adolescent in the treatment planning process, offers an aftercare program for both the child and the family, provides education and recreation programs, and involves the treatment peer group in the therapeutic process. Staff members should have credentials in addictions counseling and child development.

Contact your child's school and speak with someone in the Student Assistance Program (SAP) for a referral to an adolescent treatment center. The SAP may also offer support groups, relapse prevention programs for recovering students, and provide you with a list of young people's Alcoholics Anonymous meetings in your hometown. In addition, we've listed a few adolescent treatment centers we are personally familiar with in the Tools section.

Intervening on Someone More Than Fifty-Five Years Old

If the alcoholic is an older adult, age fifty-five or older, you need additional information before proceeding with an intervention. Symptoms of alcoholism can mirror symptoms of aging. These symptoms include shakiness, frequent falls, excessive napping, depression, reduced interest in food, isolation, dizziness, confusion, memory loss, bruising, incontinence, and poor hygiene. Alcoholism is sometimes misdiagnosed as Alzheimer's disease, stroke, or Parkinson's disease.

Family and friends must recognize that the consequences of an alcohol or other drug problem are different for the older adult. Since many older adults are retired, drive less, live away from family and friends, are financially independent, and drink alone at home, they don't experience the same kinds of consequences as a younger person. When you write your letter to the older adult, you must shift your thinking when you are looking for examples of negative consequences. A younger person may have a drunken driving arrest, threat of job loss, financial problems, or divorce. These consequences are less likely to occur in the older adult's life.

It's a good idea to contact the older adult's doctor when planning an intervention. The doctor may have no idea that the health problems of the older adult are symptoms of an underlying alcohol or prescription drug problem. It is not uncommon for doctors to misdiagnose or under-diagnose addiction in older adults even though it is a significant and growing health problem. The U.S. House of Representatives Select Committee on Aging has found that 70 percent of all hospitalizations of older adults are related to alcohol or mood-altering prescription drugs. One in five hospitalized older adults has a diagnosis of alcoholism. Alcohol is the drug of choice for the elderly.

A doctor may unwittingly contribute to the problem by prescribing sedatives, pain pills, or tranquilizers. The older adult may mix mood-altering medications with alcohol, increasing the likelihood of addiction and creating a potentially deadly combination.

The older adult may also have several doctors prescribing mood-altering drugs. If you can, look at the prescription bottles for names of prescribing physicians and pharmacies. This will help you determine if the older adult is using multiple doctors to get more drugs and shopping at different pharmacies to avoid getting caught.

If the older adult has a limited budget to cover the costs of medications, he or she may stop buying drugs that are not mood-altering in favor of spending money on medications that produce a high. For example, blood pressure pills may be abandoned in favor of tranquilizers and sedatives. The older adult's doctor can ask the pharmacy for a computer printout of the prescriptions being filled to determine if this is a problem.

Ask the doctor to write a letter recommending treatment. A family member can read the letter at the intervention. Older adults usually respond favorably to the authority of the medical profession. If prescription drugs are the problem, a doctor's letter will also counteract objections such as, "I can't be addicted to these drugs because they are prescribed by my doctor."

Before contacting the older adult's physician, go back to "Involving Doctors and Other Professionals" in section 3 and review suggestions we have made about talking with doctors. Remember, addiction is a specialized field and most doctors do not have extensive experience in this area. When you speak with the doctor, be brief and offer clear examples of the problem. It's a good idea to write down what you want to say prior to making the phone call. In most cases, the doctor is going to respond more positively if you present precise information in a short amount of time. Be clear about what it is you are asking the doctor to do. For instance, you might say: "Dr. Smith, the members of my family and I believe our seventy-nine-year-old mother, who is your patient, has an alcohol and prescription drug problem. We have found her passed out during the middle of the day. She is increasingly confused and has fallen on several occasions. We have begun monitoring her alcohol consumption by counting the bottles she throws away, and we think it's reasonable to say she drinks a pint of vodka every day. She is mixing alcohol with Valium prescribed by two different doctors. We believe this has been a problem for several years, but is getting much worse. We are planning, as a family, to ask her to go into treatment. We would like you to write a letter supporting treatment as a necessity for her well-being and health. Would you be willing to write that letter and mail it to me before we speak with her next Wednesday?"

Once the older adult is in treatment, call and inform the doctor. With a signed release of information, the treatment center can send the doctor a summary of treatment and aftercare recommendations. It is imperative the doctor understand that the older adult should not be prescribed mood-altering drugs except when absolutely necessary, such as in managing acute pain. Do not assume doctors won't prescribe mood-altering drugs to recovering alcoholics and addicts. We once worked with an elderly woman whose doctor sent her to treatment because of her twenty-five-year addiction to prescription drugs. Within two weeks after her discharge from treatment, the same doctor gave her a prescription for sleeping pills and told her, "Now you know how to keep this under control so we shouldn't have any future problems." The doctor didn't understand that recovery requires abstinence, and addicted people can't learn to use drugs in the controlled way nonaddicted people use them.

Intervening on older adults requires sensitivity to their heightened sense of shame about alcohol or other drug problems. They grew up believing alcoholism is caused by weak character and moral failings. For this reason, avoid words such as alcoholic, alcoholism, addict, and addiction during the intervention. These words create pictures of skid row bums in the minds of many older adults. These words can trigger their defenses and create feelings of shame. It's far better to say something like this: "Mom, I've seen alcohol have an increasingly negative impact on your life. You've had falls. You shake in the morning. You have frequent lapses of memory. I found you unconscious on the living room floor last Thursday. This isn't unusual for people as they get older and their bodies change. They can't handle alcohol in the same way anymore. We know that alcohol problems sneak up on people in their later years without them realizing it. The American Medical Association knows this is a disease that responds to professional treatment. I'm here today to ask you to get help for the alcohol problem affecting your health."

You'll notice that this example addresses alcoholism as a medical issue. It mentions the American Medical Association, describes the problem as common among people in later life, and explains that physical changes affect how older people handle alcohol. All these things help reduce the older person's shame. Feeling less shame, they will be less defensive during the intervention.

When selecting a treatment center, look for a program designed for older adults. They have special needs that may be overlooked in treatment programs designed for younger people. Older adults require a longer detox, need scheduled rest periods during the day, take more time to get around between appointments, and make slower progress in treatment. Older adults have a hard time relating to the younger drug addict, resist participating in group therapy, don't respond well to direct confrontation, and need daily one-on-one contact with their counselors. They also have many grief issues specific to their age. Older adult treatment programs are designed to meet these special needs. If there are no older adult programs in your local area, we've listed a few in the Tools section.

It may take older adults longer to recover, but they are more successful in treatment and recovery than any other age group. Once they are released from the grips of alcohol or other drugs, the changes are nothing less than miraculous. They recapture their life and vitality. We've heard so many people say, "Well, they're old. Let them drink. It's the one thing they enjoy." Alcoholism or addiction to other drugs is never enjoyable at any age.

We had a seventy-two-year-old grandmother as a patient several years ago. She came into treatment malnourished, bruised from head to toe, shaky, and confused. She was mixing alcohol with prescription mood-altering drugs. A neighbor found her passed out in her driveway one morning. Her kids didn't trust her with the grandchildren anymore. She stopped going out with friends. She didn't eat, shower, or clean her house. There is nothing romantic about this picture. Once she got into recovery, her life changed. Her family came together again, she enjoyed her grandchildren, and she began traveling. She sent us postcards from her snorkeling adventure in the Caribbean and her hiking trip in the mountains of Arizona. This was a woman who could barely walk when she came into treatment. With recovery, she was free to enjoy the true gifts of life.

Family involvement in treatment is always important, but especially so in the case of older adults. Attend the family program and speak to the counselors regularly. The older adult will have struggles in treatment, and you can provide valuable help to the clinical staff. You'll need a clear understanding of the aftercare recommendations the older adult must follow after leaving treatment. The clinical team will help the family identify ways it can support the older adult in early recovery and beyond. Older adult programs are designed to initiate a high level of family involvement throughout the treatment process.

What an Intervention Looks Like

Let's take a glance at what an actual intervention looks like. The next several pages guide you through a typical intervention that we've re-created to give you a clear picture of what you'll probably experience. You will read how the chairperson handles objections, how team members deliver their bottom lines, and how the intervention is concluded.

As a rule, interventions unfold just as our prototype. The alcoholic rarely interrupts the members of the team as they read their letters, almost never walks out during the intervention, and, in practically every case, will become tearful rather than angry. Eight-five percent of the time, the alcoholic or addict agrees to accept help.

Since we can't predict with complete accuracy whether a particular intervention will end with an agreement to accept help, we must be prepared for all possible outcomes. For this reason, we offer different endings to our sample intervention.

When the alcoholic is adamant about refusing help and won't be swayed by bottom lines, we can suspend the rule that the chairperson alone speaks to the alcoholic. While we never dissolve into free-for-all arguments during interventions, a few well-chosen words from a team member with significant influence may help change the alcoholic's mind. This is a last resort effort and your team must play this one by ear. Stay true to the rule that no one resorts to anger, blame, or admonishment, and you should be all right. If it's clear that you are not getting anywhere, end the intervention. Ultimately, you must preserve the alcoholic's dignity and leave the door open to future opportunities.

Intervention: A Portrayal

Characters

Greg, *a thirty-five-year-old with an alcohol problem*
Audrey, *his seventy-nine-year-old grandmother*
Rose, *his mother*
Katie, *his younger sister, and the detail person*
Janet, *his wife*
Ashley, *his thirteen-year-old daughter*
Ken, *his best friend, and the chairperson*
Judy, *his workplace supervisor, unable to attend*

The intervention is taking place in the living room of Greg's grandparents' home. Greg was told that the family is gathering there for a Sunday brunch. Greg is expected to arrive with his wife, Janet, and daughter, Ashley, at 10:00 A.M. The other family members will arrive thirty minutes earlier.

Greg's supervisor, Judy, could not attend but wrote a letter for the intervention. Her letter is read by Ken.

Greg is not expecting his best friend, Ken, to attend the brunch, so Ken parks his car in a discreet location.

A day earlier, during the rehearsal, the team drew up a seating plan for the intervention. Everyone is seated in their places before Greg arrives. Greg's wife and daughter will immediately go to their assigned seats upon entering the grandparents' home. Ken, as chairperson, will greet Greg and escort him to the seat the team has preselected for him.

Greg has a devoted relationship to his mother, Rose, and his best friend, Ken. Therefore, he is seated between the two of them. Greg is seated away from the door. To leave the intervention, he'll have to walk past his best friend, his daughter, and his grandmother. Greg has deep respect for his grandmother and great love for his daughter. The two of them are seated together to create a strong emotional force. Greg and his wife, Janet, love each other, but their relationship is filled with anger. For this reason, Janet is seated across the room from Greg. Putting space between Greg and his wife helps prevent angry interactions. Greg has always been close to his sister, Katie, so she is seated next to Janet to help neutralize the anger between Janet and Greg.

The time is 9:45 A.M. The members of the intervention team take their seats in the living room. Greg, his wife, and daughter are expected to arrive in fifteen minutes. All beverages, food, and cigarettes are put away

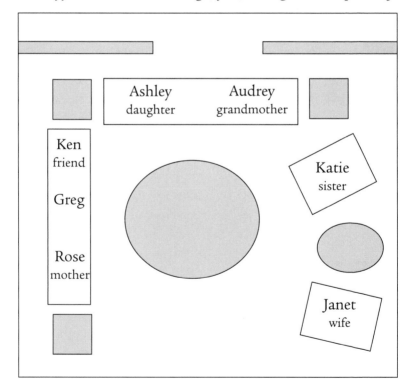

before the intervention begins. Telephone ringers, cell phones, and pagers are turned off. The team waits, listening for the sound of Greg's car pulling into the driveway. When they hear a car pull up and car doors slam, Ken, as chairperson, gets up to greet Greg at the door. The doorbell rings, and Ken opens the door.

GREG: [*surprised*] Ken, what are you doing here?

Janet and Ashley walk past Ken and go to their seats in the living room.

KEN: [*warmly, putting his hand on Greg's shoulder and looking him straight in the eye*] Greg, your family loves you very much and so do I. We've come together today because we have some important things we want to share with you. Come on in with me.

Ken's hand moves from Greg's shoulder to his back, gently guiding Greg toward the living room.

KEN: [*gesturing toward the couch where Rose is seated*] Here. Take a seat next to your mom.

Greg sits down next to his mother and Ken sits down next to Greg. Greg looks around the room at everyone. The room is silent.

GREG: [*tentatively*] Hey, how's everyone doing? What's going on?

KEN: [*calmly*] Greg, we're all doing just fine today. We've gotten together because each of us has taken some time to write you a letter, and we'd like to share them with you. We ask you to just listen as we read, and your sister would like to read her letter first.

Katie looks up at her brother and after a two-second pause begins to read her letter.

KATIE: [*crying, takes a moment to compose herself before beginning to read*] Dear Greg, You're my big brother, and I've looked up to you my whole life. You were always the smartest and the funniest of anybody. You don't know how proud I was to tell people you were my big brother. I always felt like I was something just because I was related to you. I was so shy growing up, and you were always there to take me under your wing. Like when I had that huge crush on Billy Olson, and you started inviting him over to play touch football just so I could get to know him. You've always put other people before yourself. It is this generosity of your spirit that I so admire. I don't say it nearly enough but I love you more than anything.

Katie finishes her letter by talking about the alcohol problems she's witnessed firsthand and by asking Greg to accept help today. Greg stares down at his hands. Ken glances at Janet to cue her that it's her turn to read her letter.

JANET: Dearest Greg, You are my husband and my best friend.

Greg's demeanor stiffens as Janet begins to speak. His eyes flash with anger as he looks up at her.

When I first met you, I was so infatuated with you. You made me laugh all night long. You have the funniest sense of humor. But more importantly, your warm heart and compassion for others shines through everything you say and do. That's as true today as it was then. It's what I love most about you still. I know we've had some hard times lately, but don't ever doubt my love for you. I'm so sorry for all of the harsh and unloving things I've said to you. I just didn't know what to do, and I let my anger take over. But you must know that it's the depth of my love for you and my devotion to our marriage that I've been fighting for—I don't want to lose you. I love you too much.

Janet finishes her letter by talking about the alcohol problems she's witnessed firsthand and by asking Greg to accept help today. Greg's jaw is set and he looks at her accusingly. Ken glances at Audrey, Greg's grandmother, to cue her that it's her turn.

AUDREY: [*gazes at Greg steadily for a few seconds and then reads her letter*] Dear Gregory, I was with your mother when she went into labor with you, and I drove her to the hospital. Your dad showed up a few minutes later, and I sat with him in the waiting room, calming his nerves. When the nurse came out holding you in her arms, the first thing your dad asked was, "Is Rose all right?" When the nurse assured him that your mom was just fine, he looked down at you with so much pride. The nurse said, "It's a boy. You have a son." Your dad started crying like a baby right then and there. If your dad was still with us today—and I think he is looking down on us right now—he'd tell you that you were his whole world. [*starts to cry*] He loved you with his heart and soul. He'd do anything for you. And so would I. After all, you were my boy from the start. The first time I held you, you looked up at me and the biggest smile lit across your face. I knew it was an instant bond between you and me.

Audrey finishes her letter by talking about the alcohol problems she's witnessed firsthand and by asking Greg to accept help today. Greg's head is in his hands and tears are running down his cheeks. Ken nods at Rose, Greg's mother, to cue her that it is her turn.

ROSE: [*crying softly as she begins to read*] Dear Greg, I'm so proud of you, Son, for everything you've accomplished in your life. From the very beginning you've been a ray of sunshine in my life. When you were three, and I was pregnant with Katie, you asked me where babies came from. I told you that if God smiled down on a mommy and daddy, they got a baby. God definitely smiled the day you were born. He gave you a kind and generous heart, and the gift of laughter. I've always felt that you were a wonderful gift to me. When your father died, you were my strength. You came to see me every single day. You took care of the house, the car, and the yard. You made me laugh when I thought I would never laugh again. If it hadn't been for you, I don't think I could have gotten through that first year after your father's death. Son, I love you more than life itself.

Rose finishes her letter by talking about the alcohol problems she's witnessed firsthand and by asking Greg to accept help today. Greg nods yes to her request, tears in his eyes. Ken nods to Ashley, Greg's daughter, who begins reading her letter.

ASHLEY: [*looks at her dad and then down at her letter*] Dear Dad, I think you must be the best dad anybody could ever have. We always have a lot of laughs kidding around, and you always think of the most fun things to do. When I want to get permission to do something, I always ask you, because—like Mom says— you're the softie and can never say no. I love you so much, Dad. [*starts crying and takes several deep breaths to compose herself before reading again*] But lately things have been different. You and Mom fight all the time, and I've seen you drunk. It scares me. I know you don't mean it, and it's not really you. I've learned that this is a disease and it takes help to get better. I want you to get better. I want to have a happy life for all of us. Please, Dad, accept help today. I love you. Your daughter, Ashley.

GREG: [*crying*] I love you too, Pumpkin. I love you too.

KEN: [*turns toward Greg and begins to read*] Dear Greg, We've been best friends since the ninth grade. That's twenty-one years now. You were always the guy ready to try anything. You've never let anything get in your way when you wanted to accomplish something. I may not have told you this before, but you have always been an inspiration to me. I've pushed myself harder to accomplish more in my life because of the example you've set.

You were best man at my wedding, and you're my son's godfather. This makes you more than my best friend—you're a member of my family. The kids call you "Uncle Greg," and they love you very much. Lately, however, they've asked me what's wrong with you. The last several times you've been over you've gotten pretty intoxicated, and the kids have been a little frightened of you. You get too loud and your play becomes too aggressive. The kids have always adored you, but the alcohol changes you. We've explained to them that you have an alcohol problem and that it's an illness. Christopher asked us why nobody was helping you. At that moment I realized that I was avoiding you more and more when I should be helping you instead. I promised Chris I would do whatever I could to help.

That is why I am here today. I've always considered myself a good friend to you, but I've known for some time that alcohol is a problem in your life and I chose to look the other way. That's not what friends do. Today I am willing to do the tough thing and ask you to accept treatment for your alcohol problem. We've made all of the arrangements for you to check into a treatment center today. Greg, will you accept the help we are offering you? Your friend, Ken

Silence

KEN: [*looking directly at Greg*] Greg, are you willing to go into treatment today? We have made all the arrangements at an excellent treatment center. Everything is taken care of for you.

GREG: [*composing himself*] You're probably right. I might have a problem. But I can't go anyplace today. We're in the middle of a big project at work, and it's not as if I can just disappear from my job. Maybe in a month I'll go. But, really, I think I can handle this on my own. I promise you all that I won't drink anymore. Not a drop.

KEN: [*calm and steady*] In the past, you've gone on the wagon. That's been an attempt to control this problem, but it hasn't worked. We've learned that recovery requires accepting help from others.

Also, we have a letter from your supervisor, and she asked us to read it to you. She writes: "Dear Greg, Our company has a policy that supports treatment for alcohol problems. I have made arrangements for your medical leave. The only thing you need to do is to make a phone call to me once you've been admitted into treatment. You can be assured that the reason for your leave will be kept confidential and your job will be waiting for you upon completion of treatment. On a more personal note, I have a son who is recovering from alcoholism, so I have an intimate understanding of this problem. Please know that I support you in your decision to accept help today. Sincerely, Judy."

Silence

GREG: [*deep sigh*] I guess I don't have much choice. Okay, I'll go. But how long do I have to stay?

KEN: Greg, that is for your treatment team to decide. We are asking you to follow their recommendations because they know how much time you'll need in treatment. Will you agree to follow their recommendations?

GREG: [*nods*] Yeah. I will.

KEN: [*smiling*] I think I can speak for everyone in this room when I say we're really proud of you.

Everybody gets up and hugs Greg. Ken and Katie walk Greg out to the car. Greg's suitcase is already in the trunk. Greg, Ken, and Katie leave. Rose calls the treatment center's admissions department to tell them Greg has agreed to accept help and is on his way. Everybody leaves to join Greg, Ken, and Katie at the treatment center.

A Different Ending

The scenario you just read ended positively, but sometimes alcoholics and addicts refuse to accept help. When this happens, the chairperson introduces the bottom lines just as Ken does below.

Ken asks Greg to accept help, and Greg refuses.

> GREG: [*annoyed*] I have too many things going on right now and my answer is no. I am not going to treatment. That is my final answer.

> KEN: [*calmly*] Each of us in this room loves you very much. For that reason, none of us is willing do anything that will continue supporting your alcohol problem. We've also decided that if you do not choose treatment, we must take care of ourselves. We've all decided what that means for us. We'd like to share our decisions with you. Your sister will begin.

> KATIE: [*reading*] Greg, I love you so much that I can't bear to watch you self-destruct. I'm no longer willing to pretend everything is all right, because it isn't. If you decide not to get help, I will no longer look the other way when you drive drunk. I'd never be able to forgive myself if you killed yourself or someone else. I can't stand by and do nothing anymore. As difficult as it will be, I will call the police if I see you drive drunk. Please get help so it never comes to that.

GREG: [*impatiently*] Listen. I can handle this problem on my own. Besides, I don't think this is anybody's business. This is my life, and I'm not hurting anybody.

KEN: [*calmly*] You've tried to handle it on your own before without success. We've taken time to learn about this problem, and we now know that recovery requires getting outside help. And it is our business. Each of us has been hurt by this problem. It affects all of us more than you can know. Now let's hear what your grandmother has to say. [*nods to Audrey*]

AUDREY: [*reading*] Gregory, I love you, but I've always been straight with you. Your drinking has caused your grandfather and me a lot of concern and worry. When you show up in the morning smelling of liquor, it's really hard on your grandfather. Especially since his stroke. His health can't take the worry. Until you do the right thing and get the help you need, you can't come to the house. As long as you refuse help, you're telling me that alcohol is the most important thing in your life and that hurts me. I feel I'm playing second fiddle to a bottle of booze. It's time you make a choice about what's really important in your life. Won't you accept help today?

ROSE: [*reading*] Greg, I've learned that I've enabled you to continue drinking. I'm not proud of it, and I've vowed to stop doing it. I've let you stay at my house when you and Janet have fights, and many times you've shown up drunk. I've cleaned you up, put you to bed, fed you in the morning, and never said much about the drinking. I've let you come home whenever you want, making it easy for you to run from the responsibilities of your family. I'm ashamed to say that I've even blamed Janet for your problems when it's really the drinking. I'm not going to bail you out anymore. If you get thrown out of the house, you'll either have to get help for your drinking or find another place to stay. I won't help you while you're drinking anymore, but I will help you if you want to get better. Will you accept help today?

KEN: [*reading*] You're my best friend and you can always call me if you change your mind and decide to get help. I'll pick you up and drive you to treatment anytime. But I'm going to ask that you don't stop by the house until you get help. If you choose alcohol over treatment, you can't be around the kids. They've already been affected by your drinking problem, and their welfare is a priority. It doesn't mean we don't love you. It means we are deciding how to take care of ourselves. Won't you take care of yourself and get help today?

JANET: [*reading*] Greg, as much as I want to save our marriage, I can't live with your drinking anymore. If you decide not to get help, I have to think about Ashley and myself. We can't keep living like this. Until you get help, you need to find another place to live. If you want to drink, you can't live in our house any longer starting today. But if you choose help, I'm willing to do my part, too. I know we could rebuild our marriage if the alcohol was no longer an issue. Will you please accept help?

ASHLEY: [*reading*] Dad, Mom talked to me about her decision to ask you to leave the house. I don't think I've ever cried so hard. I never thought this would happen to us. I don't want our family to break up, but I understand why Mom is doing what she's doing. Our life at home has been pretty bad. Won't you go to treatment instead? [*begins to cry*] I told Mom you'd get help if we asked.

KEN: Greg, we'll all stand by you if you reach out for help. Will you accept the help we're offering you today?

GREG: [*visibly shaken*] I need a minute to think. Grandma, is there any coffee out in the kitchen?

AUDREY: Yes. There's some in the pot.

Greg gets up and walks into the kitchen.

KEN: [*quietly, to the team*] Everybody stay seated and remain quiet. Let him have some time to think.

After several minutes pass, Ken motions to Audrey.

KEN: [*quietly*] Maybe you should go check on him.

Audrey gets up and goes into the kitchen to talk to Greg.

AUDREY: How're you doing?

Greg shrugs his shoulders.

I know we're asking you to do something you don't want to do. It's not about wanting to go, Greg. It's about needing to go. One thing I've learned about life, success usually requires doing things we don't want to do. This is going to take guts. It may be the toughest thing you ever do. You're going to have to say yes when everything in you wants to say no. [*putting a hand on his shoulder and looking him in the eye*] Are you ready to do what you need to do?

GREG: [*sighs deeply*] Okay, Grams, okay. I'll do it.

AUDREY: [*patting his cheek and smiling*] Let's go tell the others.

Together, they walk out of the kitchen back toward the living room.

A Variation to the Ending

Every so often the alcoholic or addict steadfastly adheres to her decision not to accept help even after the bottom lines are read. Sometimes this happens because the alcoholic doesn't believe her family members and friends will follow through with their bottom lines. Other times, the alcoholic has become emotionally withdrawn from the family and is no longer influenced by what they think or say. Occasionally the alcoholic has been drinking before the intervention, making it difficult to break through her denial.

This is a good time to invite the alcoholic to tell the group why she won't accept help. Listen to her closely. She may provide the information you need to help her change her mind. If not, the chairperson closes the intervention as Ken does below:

> KEN: We accept the fact that getting help is ultimately your decision, and we respect that. We've told you the decisions we've made for ourselves and ask that you respect them as well. [*pause*] The last thing I have to say is that we came together today out of our love for you.

The chairperson should stand after closing the intervention, cueing everyone else to do the same. The alcoholic or addict will usually leave at this point. It's a good idea for the treatment team to reassemble and discuss their feelings with each other. Pay special attention to children who've participated in the intervention. They need to hear that they did a good job and that the alcoholic's refusal to accept help doesn't mean she doesn't love them. It's a good idea for someone to spend the night with the spouse and children of the alcoholic. In the last scenario where Greg refuses help, Janet and Ashley plan to spend the night with Katie and Rose in case Greg returns drunk or angry.

Whenever an alcoholic refuses help, it doesn't mean she won't ever choose recovery. It just means the process is going to take longer. This is when faith counts. You can't see what's ahead but you've initiated change through your intervention. Stay with your plan. Keep a loving mind-set, follow through with bottom lines, and make decisions as a team. If you do, there's a very good chance the alcoholic will go into treatment or Alcoholics Anonymous yet.

Helping without a Family Intervention

If you aren't ready for a full family intervention right now but want to do something to help the alcoholic, there are a couple of other options. Statistically, the following techniques don't have the high success rate of family intervention but are worthwhile alternatives.

The method recommended by Al-Anon is to detach from the problem, begin your own program of recovery, and stop enabling the alcoholic. Some people call this *soft intervention*. When you stop helping the alcoholic avoid the consequences of his addiction and his troubles begin stacking up, he may eventually decide to go to an Alcoholics Anonymous meeting or into treatment. No one can predict when or if this will happen. Every situation is different. But some people estimate that the success rate of soft intervention is about 50 percent. If the alcoholic never chooses recovery, you will at least succeed in your own recovery by practicing the principles of Al-Anon.

Another way to approach the alcoholic is to calmly tell him you are concerned about his drinking and to ask if he wants help. As we discussed earlier, talking to the alcoholic one-on-one is not highly effective but there are things you can do to increase your chances of success. Talk to the alcoholic when he's sober and in a receptive mood. Approach him with love and concern. Don't resort to anger or engage in debate. Follow the same guidelines used for intervention, but don't write a letter or go into a long discussion about the addiction. Instead say something like:

"Meg, you're my best friend. I value your friendship beyond all others. For this reason, I feel I must talk with you about the toll alcohol is taking on your health. I believe it's causing serious problems in your life. I'm afraid for you and don't want to lose you. Would you be willing to talk to a counselor about it? I'll go with you if you like."

If the alcoholic says no, drop it. Don't try to cajole or plead. Simply say, "Okay, I just want you to know I love you. If you ever want to talk about this, you know you can come to me." You'll have a more profound effect on the alcoholic by respecting her response to your offer for help. This will keep the door open for future opportunities.

If the alcoholic agrees to get help, be prepared to respond immediately. Have the name and telephone number of an addictions counselor in your pocket. Pull it out and say, "I took the time to find a good counselor. Her name is Carolyn Johnson, and I have her number right here. I'll give her a call. She said she had an opening this afternoon." The sooner you get the alcoholic to the counselor, the less likely she'll change her mind about going.

A third approach is to wait until something else intervenes on the alcoholic or addict and then to take action. The intervention might be a drunken driving arrest, drug bust, job loss, divorce, hospitalization, or any number of things. Any unplanned intervention caused by a negative consequence can open a door of opportunity for you. The alcoholic will be more receptive to treatment when she's in trouble. The bigger the trouble, the more receptive she'll be. Approach the alcoholic at the peak of the crisis rather than waiting until the trouble subsides. Once pain diminishes, denial snaps back into place. When crisis is the intervention, timing is everything.

SECTION

5

After the Intervention

Talking to People Who Did Not
Take Part in the Intervention

Are there significant people in the alcoholic or addict's life who you did not include on the intervention team? Did you decide not to include them because you felt they were not appropriate for an intervention? Will any of these people do things to help the alcoholic get out of treatment? If so, you may need to contact them after the intervention.

Some people may think the best way to help the alcoholic is to spring him from treatment, give him a free place to stay, lend him money, and even provide him with drinks or other drugs. These are people the alcoholic may turn to if he decides to leave treatment early. It is often prudent to call people who may try to "rescue" the alcoholic before the alcoholic calls them. Tell potential enablers that the alcoholic checked into treatment after the family asked him to get help. Explain that he may have a tough time and could decide to leave before completing the program. Make sure they understand the seriousness of this possibility. Let them know that you believe the alcoholic may turn to them for help if prematurely leaving treatment. Take the time to explain how this could seriously hurt the alcoholic. Tactfully suggest a way they can respond to the alcoholic's request for help and still be a friend. We suggest something like: "I'd love to help you out, you know that. But your family called and asked me not to get involved in this problem. They are really worried about you. If you want to leave treatment, I think you have to work that out with them." By implicating the family as the reason he or she can't help, the friend is off the hook.

We worked with a family who decided not to include one of the alcoholic's brothers on the intervention team because he had his own drinking problem. The family thought he might warn the alcoholic about the upcoming intervention. After the alcoholic was admitted into treatment, the mother called the brother. She purposely did not use the word *intervention* during the conversation because she thought he might have false ideas about what that meant. Instead she said: "The family got together today and talked to Leon about his drinking. We asked him to get help. We waited until now to tell you because the two of you are so close. We didn't want to put you in the middle." The brother surprised everyone by responding, "It's about time someone talked to him. His drinking is out of control." When the mother asked the brother not to help the alcoholic leave treatment early, he readily agreed.

Some people may not want the alcoholic to get sober. An addicted spouse, girlfriend, or boyfriend will view treatment as a threat. Alcohol or other drug use is the essence of their relationship, and when one person gets sober the relationship doesn't work anymore. Some families in this situation intervene on both addicted people. This requires two separate interventions that take place one right after the other. We recently intervened on a husband and wife. The members of the first intervention team were from the husband's family. The husband's employer was on the team, too, so the intervention took place in his office. When the husband agreed to treatment, his family drove him to a local facility. The members of the second intervention team were from the wife's family. They went to the wife's house and intervened on her. When they told her that the husband was on his way to treatment, she agreed to accept help. The family drove her to a different treatment center in a nearby city.

If a double intervention isn't possible, notify the treatment team about the addicted partner. Also tell them about drinking buddies that might cause problems, or other people who may enable the alcoholic. If counselors have this information, they can help the alcoholic examine destructive relationships and understand why they're incompatible with sobriety. You can't control what the alcoholic does, but you can open the doors of communication so that problems don't remain secrets. Resolving problems requires bringing them out in the open.

Sending Your Intervention Letters to the Counselor

Intervention letters can be powerful therapeutic tools during the early treatment experience. After the intervention, the detail person should collect all the letters and send them to the treatment center. Don't send bottom lines with the letters. Bottom lines play a separate role which we'll discuss in a later chapter.

Before mailing or delivering letters to the treatment center, call and ask for the name of the alcoholic or addict's counselor. The treatment staff can give you this information only if the alcoholic has signed a release of information form. Without this release, they are not allowed to share any information. In this case ask for the name of the clinical director. Send the letters to him or her with a request that they be forwarded to the counselor.

If the alcoholic has refused to sign a release form that gives the counselor permission to talk to family members, don't let that stop you. You can provide the counselor with information even if he or she can't talk with you. Call the treatment center and say, "I know the federal laws on confidentiality do not permit you to say whether Jane Smith is or is not a patient at your facility. However, that does not prevent me from talking to you. May I please talk to any counselor available at this time?" Counselors have very little free time. You may have ten minutes or less before the counselor has to leave for an appointment, so prepare yourself. Write down the most important points on paper before you call.

Intervention letters can help the alcoholic work through

anger. Carol Colleran, director of the Older Adult Program at the Hanley-Hazelden Center in West Palm Beach, Florida, told us that her patients read intervention letters during a counseling session in her office. She then asks them to read one or two letters during a group therapy session and ask for group feedback. She reports that group members often express thoughts such as, "Your family must love you very much to do what they have done. I wish my family had done the same for me." Feedback from the group can help move alcoholics out of anger and into acceptance. Acceptance is the first step toward gratitude.

Intervention letters help break through denial. In treatment, most alcoholics and addicts minimize, rationalize, and deny their drug problems. Even if the consequences of addiction are severe, the addict may have difficulty seeing the problem clearly. Counselors and other patients can point out the discrepancies between the alcoholic's account of his drug problem and his family's account reported in the intervention letters.

When an entire group of people identifies addiction as the problem, the implication is too great for most alcoholics to ignore. For example, if one person comes up to you and says your nose is green, you'll probably laugh it off as a prank. But if several different people come up to you and comment on your green nose, you'll head for the nearest mirror to look. Intervention letters can do the same for the alcoholic. With so many people acknowledging the problem, the alcoholic takes a second look at what is happening in his life.

Include a note to the counselor with the letters. Some counselors may not have experience using intervention letters as therapeutic tools. For this reason, the following example offers some suggestions:

Dear Ms. Counselor:

   I am writing regarding my wife, Jane Smith. As a family, we used intervention to motivate Jane to accept treatment for her cocaine problem. During the intervention, each of us read a letter

Understanding What Goes On during Treatment

Most people know about treatment, but few can describe what it is. When an alcoholic or addict goes into an inpatient treatment center, families and friends often have no idea what to expect. An alcoholic's account of treatment can vary depending on her attitude. Some alcoholics refuse to give the treatment staff permission to talk with family members, leaving the family without a reliable source for information. So let's take a look at what happens in many inpatient treatment centers. Keep in mind that programs vary and not all programs will match our example.

When the addict enters treatment, she is monitored by the medical staff until she is medically stable. She's given a physical exam by the doctor, including blood and urine screenings. The nurses check her vital signs to monitor withdrawal symptoms. Withdrawal from some drugs, such as alcohol or Valium, can be fatal. For this reason, doctors use medications to detox the addict safely. Other drugs, such as heroin, don't cause potentially fatal withdrawal but detox can be excruciating. In these cases medications are used to reduce the discomfort of withdrawal. Without medications, addicts are more likely to leave treatment because they cannot bear the pain of going through detox. So don't be alarmed if the addict tells you the doctor is prescribing mood-altering drugs. This is sometimes a necessary aspect of detoxification and is terminated once the alcoholic is physically stable.

Treatment centers rarely provide private rooms because alcoholics and addicts tend to isolate themselves from other people, and isolation blocks recovery. For this reason, almost everyone in treatment has a roommate. If the alcoholic calls complaining about sharing a room, remember that this is an important part of the treatment process.

Each patient is assigned to a counselor who will work with her throughout treatment. Counselors don't work alone. They are part of a clinical team including some or all of the following: a psychologist, a psychiatrist, a medical doctor, nurses, addictions counselors, clergy, relapse specialist, aftercare specialist, and activities director. The clinical team meets to discuss each patient's needs and progress. Even though the addict's primary counselor manages her case, the addict is being treated by the entire team.

In the first few days of treatment, the patient goes through an assessment process. The medical team assesses the patient's physical health and makes recommendations for health care needs. For instance, if the patient has a bladder infection, the doctor will prescribe antibiotics. Problems that don't require immediate attention will be referenced in the patient's *aftercare plan*. This aftercare plan lists everything the patient needs to do for her recovery and health after discharge from treatment. The doctor also will alert counselors to problems that might hinder progress in treatment such as hearing loss or limited mobility. These problems require immediate solutions so the patient gets the most from her treatment experience.

In some centers a psychologist does a psychological assessment, using testing and personal interviews. If problems beyond chemical dependency exist, the psychologist will inform the team of what is called a *dual diagnosis*. This means two problems exist together but neither problem causes the other. For example, a patient may have an anxiety disorder as well as chemical dependency. The psychologist or psychiatrist determines what additional clinical services are needed for patients with dual diagnosis.

The addictions counselor does an assessment of the patient's history of alcohol and drug use and her personal background, including legal, financial, marital, family, employment, and social problems. If problems are not addressed, the addict may cope poorly in early recovery and resort to using alcohol or other drugs. We're not suggesting that counselors or anyone else solve the addict's problems for her, but rather help her develop a plan for solving her own problems once she's discharged from treatment.

When the assessments are complete, the clinical team reviews the information and makes treatment recommendations. Based on these recommendations and input from the patient, the counselor writes a treatment plan. The treatment plan lists the problem areas identified by the clinical team, and then each problem is matched with a goal for treatment. To help the patient reach her treatment goals, the clinical team adds assignments to the treatment plan. The counselor monitors the patient's progress as she works on these assignments. If her work is unsatisfactory, the counselor meets with the patient to identify the problems blocking her progress.

Alcoholics and addicts often come to treatment expecting to spend most of their time talking one-on-one with a counselor. In actuality, the focus of treatment is on group sessions. The patient goes to several groups each day, but meets with her counselor individually only two or three times a week. The counselor is the patient's guide throughout treatment, but recovery happens through group interactions. So if the alcoholic calls complaining that she doesn't meet with her counselor often enough, ask her how many group sessions she has every day.

Recreation is an important activity in treatment. We've heard people scoff at treatment centers saying, "This is nothing but a country club." This statement ignores the long hours and difficult personal introspection required of people in treatment and underestimates the importance of setting aside time for fun. Alcoholics and addicts don't know how to have fun while sober, and they need to learn. If an addict is miserable and bored in sobriety, she is at greater risk for relapse. Many treatment centers offer pools, gymnasiums, game rooms, or workout centers; they employ activities directors and schedule recreation as a part of daily schedules. So if the alcoholic tells you about the great swimming pool or the terrific volleyball games, don't resent the good time she's having in treatment. She needs to practice having fun without alcohol or other drugs.

Although daily schedules of different inpatient treatment programs vary, they are more alike than different. We put together the following schedule based on our experiences. It gives you a general idea of what an alcoholic or addict does during a typical day in an inpatient treatment setting:

7:00	Morning Meditation Reading/Discussion
7:30–8:15	Breakfast
8:15–8:45	Personal Time/Work on Assignments
8:45–9:30	Lecture and Discussion
9:30–10:00	Personal Time/Work on Assignments
10:00–11:30	Group Therapy
11:40–12:15	Relapse Prevention Group
12:20–12:50	Lunch
12:50–1:15	Personal Time/Work on Assignments
1:15–2:00	Lecture and Discussion
2:10–3:00	Alcoholics Anonymous Orientation/Big Book Study
3:00–4:15	Pool or Gym
4:30–5:15	Sober Living Planning Group
5:15–5:45	Relaxation Therapy
5:45–6:30	Dinner
6:30–7:45	Lecture and Discussion
8:00–9:00	Alcoholics Anonymous Meeting
9:00–10:30	Personal Time
10:30	Lights Out

Individual sessions with an addictions counselor are scheduled during a patient's personal time. Other groups offered in many treatment programs include Grief Group, Twelve Step Study, Aftercare Planning, Nutrition Guidance, HIV/AIDS Education, and Family Program. Some treatment centers set aside Sunday afternoons for relaxation and family visitation.

Before a patient is discharged from treatment, the clinical team develops his aftercare plan. The plan outlines what the patient needs to do to maintain sobriety and successfully work through other problems in his life. Following are two examples of aftercare plans.

1. For ongoing sobriety attend four or more Alcoholics Anonymous meetings per week; ask five Alcoholics Anonymous members for their telephone numbers and talk to at least one of them daily; obtain an Alcoholics Anonymous sponsor within two weeks of discharge from treatment; work the Twelve Steps with your Alcoholics Anonymous sponsor. Attend the Aftercare Support Group every Wednesday at 6:30 P.M. for six months. Set up a credit counseling session at a nonprofit, no-cost organization by calling 555-1625. Begin marriage counseling six months after discharge from treatment or as determined appropriate by aftercare counselor. See your medical doctor, as necessary, for ongoing medical problems. Make an appointment at a pain management clinic to discuss biofeedback techniques for managing back pain.

2. Upon discharge, transfer to a halfway house program for four months. Attend Narcotics Anonymous meetings as determined appropriate by halfway house staff and obtain a Narcotics Anonymous sponsor to help you work the Twelve Steps. Follow all halfway house expectations. Seek individual counseling to deal with problems related to but beyond chemical dependency. After completion of the halfway house program, follow the

aftercare recommendations provided by the halfway house staff.

Sometimes patients refuse to comply with aftercare plans. When this happens, the clinical team holds a conflict resolution meeting with the patient. The team listens to the reasons the patient doesn't want to comply and then explains why they feel the recommendations are necessary and appropriate. They may ask the patient to discuss his reluctance with his peer group and ask them for feedback. Many patients finally agree to comply. Those who don't are at high risk of eventually returning to alcohol or other drug use.

If a patient stubbornly refuses to follow his aftercare plan, the treatment team will write a secondary aftercare plan. For instance, if a halfway house program is refused, the team may recommend an intensive outpatient program. In this case, the secondary aftercare plan does not provide as much support as the clinical team believes the alcoholic needs in early recovery, but is the next best option. When a patient refuses to attend Alcoholics Anonymous, the clinical team will not eliminate Alcoholics Anonymous from the aftercare plan. Attending a Twelve Step program is not an optional part of recovery.

Family members should be familiar with the aftercare plan recommendations before the alcoholic is discharged from the treatment facility. If the alcoholic refuses to let the counselor share aftercare planning with the family, he's probably not serious about long-term recovery.

Family involvement during treatment is very important. Counselors need family input since alcoholics often deny and minimize their problems. Without talking to families, counselors can't be certain that the information they get from patients is accurate. An alcoholic's account of his problem and his family's account are often vastly different. If the counselor doesn't contact you in the first two days of treatment, initiate the call yourself.

Preparing for Objections during Treatment

Once the alcoholic or addict is in treatment, denial often resurfaces. This happens to people whether or not they've gone through an intervention. Denial is like a punching bag. When you knock the bag down it pops right back into place. Denial acts the same way. It has to be knocked down over and over.

When denial pops back up, the alcoholic may start looking for escape routes out of treatment. You'll know when he's found one because he'll tell you about it in the form of an objection. The alcoholic will probably call a family member he thinks he can easily influence and present his objections to treatment. Some of the most common objections are:

- I understand everything they're telling me. I really don't need to stay here any longer. I know what to do. There is nothing more they can teach me.

- The people here are all worse off than I am. There's a guy who used heroin and another one was a crack addict. Get me out of this place.

- I've got important business to deal with right now. It can't wait. I've got to go.

- It's not right to be away from my kids this long. They need me. I've got to go home and take care of them.

- I can't afford treatment, and I refuse to let anyone else pay for it.

- I see the error of my ways. I'll never drink or drug again. I've really learned my lesson this time.
- The food here is terrible, and I can't sleep in a strange bed. I'm miserable, and I don't have to subject myself to this.
- They're making me share a room with two other people. I have no privacy, and I don't trust these people. I'm not going to stay in this place.
- The staff here doesn't know what they're doing. I'm not being seen enough, and my counselor is incompetent.
- This program is the pits. I'm not getting a thing out of it.

Prepare yourself for treatment objections in the same way you prepared for the intervention. Brainstorm with team members. Write down possible objections and how you'll answer them. Every team member should be prepared for the alcoholic to call with reasons why he must leave treatment early. If the alcoholic presents an objection, try one of the following answers: "I suggest you discuss that problem with your counselor," or "I don't know what to tell you. I'd recommend that you take that to your group," or "I understand that you have a problem with the food (roommate, bed, being away from the children) but your most important problem is your chemical dependency. Recovery takes precedence over all other concerns." If the alcoholic continues to object, use the broken record technique by repeating the same answer over and over again. If the alcoholic becomes angry, calmly tell him that you must end the conversation. Don't start reacting to the alcoholic's anger. If you are tempted to engage in debates or arguments, tell yourself to stop. End the conversation and call a member of the intervention team for support.

If you find yourself believing the alcoholic's objection, warning bells should go off in your head. When the alcoholic's objection begins making sense, the addiction is running the show. If this happens, slow everything down. Stop and think. You don't have to make an immediate decision. Respond by saying, "I'll have to think about that." The alcoholic will probably pressure you for an immediate answer, but don't rush into anything. Call your team members and the addictions counselor to ask for advice. By using the group to make your decisions, the alcoholic is less likely to manipulate you into doing the wrong thing. If the alcoholic won't allow you to speak with his counselor, that's a sign that he's trying to control you.

Of course an alcoholic doesn't need the family's permission to leave treatment. He can leave any time. But if the family is using influence and leverage, the alcoholic knows he will experience consequences if he leaves treatment. He'd rather convince the family that the treatment center isn't working for him, or he doesn't belong there. Then he can leave treatment with the family's blessings and avoid negative consequences. However, a family prepared for treatment objections is less susceptible to this kind of manipulation.

If an alcoholic tells you she is leaving treatment early, put your bottom lines to work. Ask the counselor if the family can come to the treatment center and do a conflict resolution with the staff. Family members can read their bottom lines to the alcoholic with the clinical team present. Of course, this is only possible if the alcoholic has signed release forms for the family members. If you can't meet with the alcoholic in treatment, read your bottom lines to her over the phone or give them to the counselor.

Once the alcoholic is in treatment, some families start blaming the treatment staff for the alcoholic's problems. Like the alcoholic, the family begins resisting the recovery process. This is often a sign that the family feels they've lost control over the situation. They don't know what to expect anymore. The alcoholic doesn't seem to be getting better. Everything is changing. Recovery is puzzling and new. As a reaction to these uncertainties, the family turns against the treatment team. When this happens, they provide the alcoholic with an excuse to leave treatment.

If you start viewing the treatment team as the problem, discuss your concerns with the alcoholic's counselor and ask for feedback. Begin looking for solutions that support recovery. Check your expectations for early recovery. Are they realistic? Are you expecting too much too fast? How are you feeling about yourself? Do you sometimes think it would be easier to go back to the way things used to be? Are you afraid the alcoholic won't need you once she gets well? If you're blaming others rather than focusing on the recovery process, something is probably making you uncomfortable. Blame becomes your refuge and blocks recovery. Make a choice to deal with uncomfortable feelings in a different way: talk to the addictions counselor; go to Al-Anon; sign up for the family program; start seeing a counselor who works with families of alcoholics and addicts. Do something that will help you make positive change in your life.

Supporting the Alcoholic or Addict during Treatment

Support the alcoholic with actions. They speak louder than words. It's one thing to tell the alcoholic or addict that you support what she's doing; it's quite another to get busy yourself. Once the alcoholic is in treatment, it's time for you to participate in the recovery process. Remember, recovery is not a spectator sport. Everybody in the family is part of the team.

The first thing to do is to sign up for the family program offered by the treatment center. Once you know the dates and times of the program, make child care arrangements and talk to your boss about taking time off work. Let nothing interfere with your attendance. We suggest that everyone who participated in the intervention participate in the family program.

As good as your intentions may be, without this education and support you will not be well prepared to deal with early recovery. You'll likely experience confusion and frustration, and the newly recovering alcoholic will probably feel alienated and misunderstood. At first, relationship problems may grow rather than lessen. In early recovery, added pressures are placed upon the family. Properly coping with these pressures demands that you learn new ways to handle the challenges. So don't think of the family program as an elective. It's a required course for family recovery.

If the alcoholic's treatment center does not offer a family program, call other local treatment centers. Many will welcome people who do not have a family member in their rehab program.

If you don't find any locally, investigate nearby cities. If you are willing to travel, contact Hazelden at 800-257-7810, the Betty Ford Center at 800-854-9211, Father Martin's Ashley at 800-799-4673, the Caron Foundation at 800-678-2332, or Crossroads at 268-562-0035.

Next, choose a Twelve Step program that's right for you: Al-Anon is for families of alcoholics; Nar-Anon is for families of people addicted to other drugs; and Families Anonymous is for both. Many members of Families Anonymous are parents of adult children with alcohol or other drug problems. Find a meeting close to your home or workplace and begin attending. Use your telephone book or call your local information operator for a listing. The appendix lists Web site addresses and telephone numbers of a variety of Twelve Step programs.

Don't forget to send cards and letters to the alcoholic while he's in treatment. Have the kids draw pictures and make their own cards. Expressing your love shouldn't stop when the intervention ends. When the mail arrives at treatment centers, patients line up hoping for letters. Be sure your loved one isn't disappointed.

Your First Al-Anon Meeting

Making the decision to go to an Al-Anon meeting can be difficult for many people. Some people feel intimidated because they don't know what to expect. Others think they don't belong or believe they can handle things on their own. Still others insist they don't have time or that it's the alcoholic's problem not theirs. And some are afraid they might run into someone they know. This is exactly how the alcoholic or addict is feeling about going to his first Alcoholics Anonymous meeting.

Just about everyone resists going to their first meeting. Knowing what to expect can help you feel more comfortable. When you walk into an Al-Anon meeting, the first thing you'll notice is that the members look like people you see at the grocery store, your church, around your neighborhood, in school, and at work. You'll find homemakers, schoolteachers, shopkeepers, college students, nurses, business owners, electricians, doctors, computer programmers, artists, salespeople, lawyers, clerks, and the list goes on. You'll find retired people, young people, middle-aged people; the rich, poor, and middle class. You'll find people who've been going to Al-Anon for years and those coming for the first time. Despite individual backgrounds, everyone at Al-Anon comes because they have been affected by someone else's drinking. Everyone at the meeting shares a common problem.

Most Al-Anon meetings are held in churches, but they are also found in hospitals, office buildings, schools, and government facilities. Al-Anon is available most days of the week and holidays.

There are morning, lunch, evening, and weekend meetings. There are men's meetings, women's meetings, and mixed meetings. There are beginners' groups. Some Al-Anon meetings are paired with Alcoholics Anonymous meetings. Most meetings are non-smoking. Some meetings offer child care. All meetings are anonymous and confidential.

When you walk into an Al-Anon meeting, look for a display of Al-Anon literature. Ask for the free packet of information for beginners. Some people prefer to listen without speaking during their first meeting; if you're invited to talk and you prefer not to, say "I'll pass." If you choose to speak, let people know it's your first meeting.

Before the meeting begins, a member will read the preamble to the Twelve Steps. This presents an overview of Al-Anon. Next, the group recites the Twelve Steps, which provide ideas and guidance for personal growth and improved relationships. Then a member may read one of the Twelve Traditions. The Traditions guide the group so it can function smoothly. Since Al-Anon is not a structured organization and individual members are not expected to follow rules, the Traditions help ensure that individual decisions don't interfere with the welfare of the group.

Once the Steps and Traditions are read, members recite the "Serenity Prayer" and begin the meeting. Some meetings are called *speaker meetings*. At a speaker meeting, an Al-Anon member will share his or her story. Stories tell how it was in the person's past, what happened to initiate change, and how it is today. Other meetings are *discussion meetings*. At some discussion meetings, the group selects a discussion topic such as "changed attitudes" or "handling difficulties." At others, the group discusses one of the Twelve Steps or an Al-Anon slogan. Examples of Al-Anon slogans include First Things First; Easy Does It; Live and Let Live; Keep It Simple; How Important Is It?

Members don't give counsel to one another during meetings. There shouldn't be any cross-talk during discussions. In other words, only talk about yourself and don't comment on or advise other members. Members learn how to solve their common problems by listening to what has worked for others. This doesn't mean you'll necessarily agree with everything you hear. Al-Anon suggests you take what you like from a meeting and leave the rest behind.

Al-Anon is about you, not the alcoholic. By attending meetings you will find support for yourself and learn to detach from the alcoholic's problems. You'll begin to identify the ways you've changed as a result of your relationship with an addicted person. Since many of these changes are incompatible with a happy, contented life, Al-Anon helps you transform defects into assets and broken relationships into healthy ones.

There are no leaders in Al-Anon. A chairperson is a volunteer who opens and closes the meeting. Nobody acts as group facilitator or counselor. Al-Anon is nonprofessional, nonreligious, and has no political affiliations. Al-Anon discourages discussions of therapy techniques, psychology, religious affiliation, non-Al-Anon literature, intervention, and treatment programs during meetings. Discussions focus on the principles of Al-Anon. This preserves the purity of the program. There are no dues for membership, but during each meeting a basket is sent around to collect donations to pay for group expenses. Most members put a dollar or two in the basket but contributions are strictly voluntary.

Before deciding if Al-Anon is right for you, attend at least six meetings. If you don't like a particular meeting, try another one. If you attend a meeting and members are giving each other advice, cross-talking, or discussing the latest pop psychologist, find another meeting. Those conversations can happen before or after meetings, but not during. Look for meetings that uphold the Twelve Traditions and stay focused on Al-Anon literature. Then make a commitment to attend at least once a week. As they say in Al-Anon, "Keep coming back. It works if you work it."

A Few Words about Alcoholics Anonymous

Alcoholics Anonymous (AA) was not developed by physicians, psychologists, or researchers. It came about as a result of the successful experiences of alcoholics who stayed sober by helping others. Before Alcoholics Anonymous, the likelihood of an alcoholic staying sober was considered nothing short of a miracle. Today, Alcoholics Anonymous helps millions of alcoholics achieve long-term, contented sobriety. Using the principles of Alcoholics Anonymous, Narcotics Anonymous does the same for people addicted to other drugs.

Alcoholics Anonymous describes itself in the following way: "Alcoholics Anonymous is a fellowship of men and women who share their experience, strength, and hope with each other that they may solve their common problem and help others to recover from alcoholism. The only requirement for membership is a desire to stop drinking. There are no dues or fees for Alcoholics Anonymous membership; we are self-supporting through our own contributions. Alcoholics Anonymous is not allied with any sect, denomination, politics, organization, or institution; does not wish to engage in any controversy; neither endorses nor opposes any causes. Our primary purpose is to stay sober and help other alcoholics to achieve sobriety."

This preamble underscores some of the most salient facts about Alcoholics Anonymous: (1) members rely on each others' "experience, strength, and hope" to stay sober; (2) Alcoholics Anonymous members are dedicated to helping others; and (3) there are no religious, political, or financial aspects to the organization.

Some people erroneously believe Alcoholics Anonymous is a religious organization. This is not the case. Alcoholics Anonymous has a spiritual dimension, but it is not religious. Spirituality in Alcoholics Anonymous is defined as the ability to reach out for help and, as a result, achieve a changed personality. Alcoholics Anonymous members turn to other alcoholics and a Higher Power for help, but Alcoholics Anonymous does not define *Higher Power* for its members. Alcoholics Anonymous explains spirituality in the pamphlet "A Newcomer Asks" this way: "The majority of AA members believe that we have found the solution to our drinking problem not through individual willpower, but through a power greater than ourselves. However, everyone defines this power as he or she wishes. Many people call it God, others think it is the AA group, still others don't believe in it at all. There is room in AA for people of all shades of belief and nonbelief."

Alcoholics Anonymous is the most important part of any recovery program. The majority of alcohol and drug rehabilitation centers base their treatment programs on the Twelve Steps of Alcoholics Anonymous. Studies show that Alcoholics Anonymous attendance is the best predictor of long-term sobriety. For the newly recovering alcoholic, working a program of recovery in Alcoholics Anonymous requires following a few guidelines:

1. *Attend meetings.* A newly recovering alcoholic should attend a minimum of four Alcoholics Anonymous meetings every week. Some Alcoholics Anonymous members recommend ninety meetings in ninety days.

2. *Choose an Alcoholics Anonymous home group.* A home group is a meeting where the alcoholic finds his Alcoholics Anonymous sponsor, volunteers for service work, and makes lifelong friends. He never misses this meeting.

3. *Get an Alcoholics Anonymous sponsor.* An Alcoholics Anonymous sponsor is a person who guides the alcoholic through the Twelve Steps. He helps the alcoholic over the rough spots of early recovery and, if the alcoholic relapses, encourages him to return to the meetings. A sponsor is not a therapist or personal financier. He doesn't solve problems for the alcoholic or lend him money. A sponsor is a recovering alcoholic who shares his experience, strength, and hope and, in doing so, points the way to a new life of contented sobriety.

4. *Follow the directions* by following the principles of Alcoholics Anonymous and just about anybody can achieve sobriety. Alcoholics who don't follow the directions are likely to drink again. As it says in the Big Book of Alcoholics Anonymous: "Rarely have we seen a person fail who has thoroughly followed our path. Those who do not recover are people who cannot or will not completely give themselves to this simple program, usually men and women who are constitutionally incapable of being honest with themselves."

There are now millions of people around the world who have found help and recovery through Twelve Step programs. The Twelve Steps translate across geographical and cultural boundaries. As Bill Wilson, the co-founder of Alcoholics Anonymous, so aptly put it: "The unique ability of each Alcoholics Anonymous to identify himself with, and bring recovery to, the newcomer in no way depends upon his learning, his eloquence, or any special individual skills. The only thing that matters is that he is an alcoholic who has found a key to sobriety."

Preparing for the Possibility of Relapse

Many families begin worrying about relapse before the alcoholic or addict even gets into treatment. These fears are not unfounded because staying sober can be very difficult for alcoholics in early recovery. However, families who have done an intervention are better prepared to handle relapse than most families. As a team, the family can use its influence and leverage to motivate the addict to get back into recovery if a relapse occurs.

Relapse begins before the recovering alcoholic ever takes the first drink or drug. Relapse is a way of thinking and acting that leads the alcoholic back to drinking. For this reason, a return to alcohol or other drugs is always preceded by relapse warning signs. Common warnings include lack of a recovery program; risky lifestyle, such as going to bars; unresolved stress; relationship problems; peer pressure to drink; cravings for alcohol or other drugs; too much unstructured time; isolation; lingering resentments; compulsive behaviors, such as overworking; overconfidence; feelings of hopelessness and defensiveness; and dropping out of treatment or Alcoholics Anonymous.

Terence Gorski answers the question, "What are some things an alcoholic or addict might do that would cause a relapse?" in his book *Passages through Recovery*: "You don't have to do anything. Stop using alcohol and other drugs, but continue to live your life the way you always have. Your disease will do the rest. It will trigger a series of automatic and habitual reactions to life's problems that will create so much pain and discomfort that a return to chemical use will seem like a positive option." Avoiding the pain and discomfort that lead to relapse requires a program of recovery. Recovery requires a willingness to do things differently.

While not all recovering people experience relapse, it is estimated that approximately 50 percent are prone to relapse during the first three months after treatment. Relapse is a sign that something is missing from the recovery program, causing the alcoholic to become increasingly uncomfortable in sobriety. Many things can create gaps in recovery programs, including trying to recover without help; not following directions or following them only part of the time; attending Alcoholics Anonymous but never getting involved; hanging out with drinking or drugging buddies; not getting enough sleep; eating poorly; participating in the program intellectually but never emotionally; and isolating from people. Addicts who decide they don't need a program of recovery underestimate the power of addiction and are at high risk for relapse.

Many newly recovering alcoholics work solid recovery programs in Alcoholics Anonymous. They go to several meetings each week. They find sponsors who help them work the Twelve Steps. They do service work at the meetings, such as greeting newcomers and making coffee. They develop friendships with other recovering people, and they read the literature published by Alcoholics Anonymous. Alcoholics who consistently do all of these things rarely relapse. If they do, they have so much support from the people in Alcoholics Anonymous that they get right back into recovery. The same holds true for addicts attending Narcotics Anonymous.

In some cases, a recovering alcoholic or addict may suffer from another problem that blocks recovery until it is properly treated. This may be an eating disorder, gambling addiction, or other psychological problem. These problems exist separately from the chemical dependency but must be addressed before successful recovery can be maintained. Jerry Boriskin, Ph.D., psychological services director for Advanced Recovery Center in Delray Beach, Florida, explains:

> Potent triggers that lead to repeated relapse often result from undiagnosed or untreated psychological issues. Over eighty percent of those with post traumatic stress syndrome, for instance, also suffer from addiction. Individuals who have experienced trauma or who suffer from conditions such as manic depression need to focus on those issues in addition to Twelve Step work if a lasting recovery is to be achieved.

If your loved one is working a strong recovery program in Alcoholics Anonymous or Narcotics Anonymous but continues to relapse, it would be wise to get further evaluation by a professional experienced in addictions and dual diagnosis. Ask the treatment center for a referral.

Families need to prepare for relapse before it happens. We highly recommend meeting with the alcoholic and her counselor to write a *relapse agreement*. Set this meeting up toward the end of treatment. Ask the alcoholic what she wants the family to do if she relapses. By asking her rather than deciding for her, you preserve her dignity and give her the opportunity to participate in this important decision. If she relapses, she's more likely to respond positively to a relapse agreement she created. The counselor will guide the alcoholic so her plan is befitting a good relapse agreement. Once the counselor and alcoholic are satisfied, ask the alcoholic to write the agreement down on paper. Then you, the counselor, and the alcoholic sign it. Each member of the intervention team should get a copy of the agreement. It will help everyone understand what to do if the alcoholic relapses. It also provides the alcoholic with a sense of accountability because she knows that the family is prepared to act if she returns to drinking or drugs. And you've accomplished this by working with the alcoholic, not against her.

Families who attend the family program and go to Al-Anon create an ambiance that supports recovery. It's more difficult for alcoholics and addicts to return to addiction when the whole family is participating in the recovery process. If the alcoholic does relapse, families attending Al-Anon are better prepared to cope with relapse in a more productive way than families that don't attend.

Having already done an intervention on your loved one, you are capable of quickly putting together an informal intervention if a relapse occurs. You can refer to your relapse agreement if you have one. You can also call the alcoholic's former counselor at the treatment center for advice. If the alcoholic isn't involved in Alcoholics Anonymous, the counselor will likely want him to return to treatment. If he has been working a solid recovery program and has a sponsor in Alcoholics Anonymous, he may just need to talk with his sponsor and go to more meetings. If you suspect another problem in addition to addiction, get a professional evaluation. Approach the alcoholic with love. Diffuse the shame of relapse by saying you understand that relapse is a symptom of addiction and a sign that he needs more support in his recovery program. Ask the alcoholic to follow the counselor's recommendations. If the alcoholic refuses, go back to your bottom lines. Explain that you won't support the disease of addiction and you must take care of yourselves.

Relapse doesn't mean the alcoholic or addict won't recover. Sometimes relapse is what helps an alcoholic finally accept that he's powerless over alcohol and other drugs. As they say in Alcoholics Anonymous, "I guess he had to do a little more research."

Using Family Intervention
for Other Problems

Family intervention was developed to help motivate alcoholics and addicts to accept help, but intervention techniques work well to help people with other problems. Many of the symptoms of chemical dependency—denial, minimizing, and rationalizing—are symptoms of other problems, and they make it difficult for families to help their loved ones. However, intervention can break through the denial associated with compulsive disorders and process addictions, such as gambling, in much the same way it does with alcoholism and drug addiction. It's also an effective tool when an older relative needs assisted living but is resistant to leaving the family home, or is no longer able to drive a car safely but refuses to surrender his or her driver's license.

If your loved one is suffering from a compulsive behavioral disorder such as sex addiction, compulsive gambling, eating disorders, computer addiction, or shopping addiction, consult with a professional specializing in that disorder to help you prepare for the intervention. Each of these disorders has its own specific characteristics and nuances that may require special handling. The following provides you with general information about some of the disorders that can be approached through intervention:

- *Compulsive gambling* adversely affects family relationships, friendships, employment, finances, school performance, and physical and mental health. Signs of a gambling problem include spending longer and longer periods of time gambling, unexplained disappearances from home or work, waging higher stakes to win back losses, gambling until there is no more money left, lying about gambling debt, stealing or other criminal activity to finance gambling or pay debts, being mentally preoccupied with gambling, negligent of family responsibilities, declining in personal care such as sleep and nutrition, and threats of suicide related to gambling problems.

- *Sex addiction* can involve a wide variety of behaviors. The addict may have one unwanted behavior or many. Sex addiction harms relationships, careers, finances, and mental and physical health. Signs of sex addiction include secrecy about sexual activities; leading a double life; involvement in sexual activities that violate deeply held spiritual or religious beliefs; sexual involvement with people not considered acceptable as partners; greater frequency and variety of sexual exploits needed to reach the same level of stimulation; disregard for dangers of sexually transmitted disease, pregnancy, violence, or arrest; preoccupation with pornography or Internet cybersex; loss of relationship with primary partner or spouse; and threats of self-destruction or suicide.

- *Compulsive overeaters* lose control over the amount of food they eat and often suffer from obesity. Overeaters experience uncontrollable eating binges, consuming large quantities of mostly junk food. They usually binge in private, do not attempt to control their weight, and are typically suffering from severe obesity. Overeating is often related to complicated emotional problems, fears, emotional pain, and stress.

- *Eating disorders* include anorexia nervosa and bulimia nervosa. The stomach, ovaries, kidneys, teeth, salivary glands, blood pressure, hormones, and electrolytes are all adversely affected by these disorders. Extreme loss of body weight can lead to death.

Anorexia is an intense fear of gaining weight, causing continual dieting and self-starvation. It usually occurs in young women in their teens. They sometimes binge-eat and purge by vomiting or using laxatives. Signs of anorexia include severe weight loss, avoiding meals with the family, obsession with diets, feeding others but depriving self of food, compulsive exercising, cessation of menstrual cycle, mood swings, constant complaints about being overweight, wearing baggy clothes to hide weight loss from others, and distorted body image.

Bulimia is a problem marked by binge eating and vomiting. Laxatives and other medications are also used to increase the rate of weight loss. Symptoms include a chaotic lifestyle, emotional and physical suffering, disappearing to the bathroom after meals, evidence of vomiting or use of medications and laxatives, concealing symptoms, fasting, loss of dental enamel, rise in dental cavities, scarred or callused hands, irregular menstrual cycles, and constipation. Bulimics often have normal body weight or are slightly overweight.

- *Compulsive shopping* leads to uncontrollable spending and unmanageable debt. Signs of compulsive shopping include feeling "high" when shopping, buying unneeded items, unable to remember what was purchased, using shopping to overcome negative emotions, buying unaffordable items and rationalizing that they "deserve it," using credit cards to stretch shopping budgets and delay the ramifications of overspending, ignoring household budgets, experiencing shopping "hangovers" of guilt and remorse, shopping alone, hiding purchases from others, lying about the amount of money spent, spending money needed for bills or necessities, and accumulating large credit card debt.

- *Compulsive indebtedness* is an addiction to irresponsible debting. Symptoms include obsession with managing debt, unrealistic solutions to debt, chronic mishandling of finances, fantasies of far-fetched business opportunities to solve financial troubles, paying off one debt with another debt, ignoring the consequences of uncontrolled debt, feelings of euphoria when getting new credit cards or loans, frequently borrowing money from friends and family, having illusions of being rescued from the debt, ruined family lives, and feelings of suicide.

- *Computer or Internet addictive disorder* affects family relationships, friendships, employment, finances, and emotional health. Symptoms include getting a "high" when on the computer, being overly attached to the computer emotionally, inability to turn off the computer, neglecting sleep to stay up all night on the Internet, experiencing cravings for the Internet, hiding computer activities at work, lying to spouse about time spent on the computer, ignoring responsibilities at home, work, or school in favor of being on the computer, neglecting personal hygiene, not eating or eating at the computer rather than with the family, Internet chat rooms replacing real-life relationships, unable to control the amount of time spent at the computer once online, and physical problems such as carpal tunnel, migraines, or backaches. Internet addictions can culminate in shopping addictions through online auction houses; gambling addictions through online gambling venues; and sex addiction through online chat rooms, sexual partners, and pornography.

If someone is suffering from multiple addictions, talk to a professional about the correct sequence in which to address the problems. For instance, alcoholism and other drug addictions almost always need treatment first. If the alcoholism is left untreated, it will block the treatment of all other problems. A professional can also help determine if the family has misdiagnosed the primary problem. The family may decide a loved one's gambling addiction is the most serious problem and ignore or minimize his cocaine addiction. But if the gambling addiction is treated first and the cocaine problem is left untreated, the addiction to cocaine will block the treatment for compulsive gambling. Educate yourself about the specific disorder you plan to intervene on so you approach your loved with facts rather than myths and misinformation. Talk to counselors, read books, and go to workshops.

Intervention is also an excellent tool for addressing elder care issues. If an older relative is no longer capable of self-care, is unwilling to consider assisted living, and is a danger to his or her safety and well-being, intervention can help motivate the older person to make a healthier and more realistic choice. Talk to a counselor specializing in geriatric issues as part of your preparation for intervention. The counselor will teach you to listen for and answer the fears your loved one is experiencing about aging, loss of independence, and giving up his or her home. The same is true if you are planning to intervene on an older person who is unable to drive safely. For older adults, giving up a driver's license can signify losing their freedom and the ability to care for themselves.

Intervention is an effective tool to help a loved one who is unable to help him- or herself. The techniques in this book are transferable and can be used to help people with addictions and problems other than chemical dependency. However, get information and professional advice about the problem you are facing before you do an intervention. There may be special considerations you need to know about before you take action. If you want to work with a professional interventionist, find one who specializes in the specific problem area you are concerned about. If that proves difficult, hire a chemical dependency interventionist who will work in tandem with a therapist knowledgeable about the disorder.

An Instrument of Love

Intervention organizes love and honesty and uses them to break through the barrier of addiction. We bring a moment of clarity to one who cannot see; promise to one with no hope. Rarely are we presented with such an opportunity. Intervention is a chance to be an instrument of love in the world. It opens doors to miracles and grace.

People say it is grace, in the end, that saves the alcoholic. Recovering people must agree, for all over the world they claim the hymn "Amazing Grace" as their own:

> Amazing grace! How sweet the sound
> That saved a wretch like me!
> I once was lost, but now am found;
> Was blind, but now I see.
>
> 'Twas grace that taught my heart to fear,
> And grace my fears relieved;
> How precious did that grace appear
> The hour I first believed.
>
> Through many dangers, toils, and snares,
> I have already come;
> 'Tis grace hath brought me safe thus far,
> And grace will lead me home.

When we've been there ten thousand years,
Bright shining as the sun,
We've no less days to sing God's praise
Than when we'd first begun.

SECTION

6

Tools

The following section is designed to help you gather, organize, and easily retrieve information as you prepare for an intervention.

Building a Team

Use this worksheet to list all of the significant people in the alcoholic's life. Write down everyone who comes to mind. You'll draw from this list when you finalize your team. Not everyone you list will necessarily participate in the intervention.

Name_____ Phone_____

Name_____ Phone_____

Name_____ Phone_____

Name_____ Phone_____

Name_____ Phone_____

Name_____ Phone_____

Name_____ Phone_____

Name_____ Phone_____

Name_____ Phone_____

Name_____ Phone_____

Name_____ Phone_____

Name_____ Phone_____

Name_____ Phone_____

Name_____ Phone_____

The Planner

Compiling and Organizing the Details

This tool is critical for the detail person and for keeping the entire group up-to-date.

The team members:

Name_____ Phone_____

Name_____ Phone_____

Name_____ Phone_____

Name_____ Phone_____

Name_____ Phone_____

Name_____ Phone_____

Name_____ Phone_____

Name_____ Phone_____

The detail person_____ The chairperson_____

Who has the most influence?_____

_____

Who has leverage?_____

_____

Dates, times, and location(s):

Rehearsal location_____ Date:_____ Time: _____

Intervention location_____ Date: _____ Time: _____

The financial details:

Insurance policy number

_____

Insurance group number

_____

Medicare, Medicaid

_____

Other financial resources

_____

_____

_____

Your treatment center choices
(see "Evaluating Treatment Centers," later in this section)

Treatment center #1:

_____

Address _____

_____

Contact person_____ Phone _____

Financial requirements

_____

Copay_____ Deductible _____

- ☐ Inpatient treatment
- ☐ Evening outpatient treatment
- ☐ Medical detox required prior to admission
- ☐ Smoking areas are provided

Admission date and time _____

What to pack _____

Family program schedule _____

Treatment center #2

_____

Address _____

_____

Contact person_____ Phone _____

Financial requirements _____

Copay_____ Deductible _____

- ☐ Residential inpatient treatment
- ☐ Evening outpatient treatment
- ☐ Medical detox required prior to admission
- ☐ Smoking areas are provided

Admission date and time

_____

What to pack _____

Family program schedule _____

Selecting a professional interventionist

Name_____ Phone _____

Address _____

_____

Fee _____

Appointment place, date, and time _____

Keeping the family involved

Schedule family program

Dates _____

Times _____

Al-Anon/Families Anonymous: Location _____

Day and time _____

Compile facts essential to the alcoholic's or addict's treatment

Each person in the family knows different things about the alcoholic's history. Working as a group, you can create a more complete picture of what has been happening. The treatment center staff will ask for this information prior to setting up the admission.

Alcoholic's address _____

_____

Phone_____ Date of birth _____

Age _____

Marital status _____

Children _____

Employment _____

Legal problems _____

Previous counseling _____

Dates _____

Previous treatment or detox _____

Dates _____

Alcoholics Anonymous attendance _____

Dates _____

Periods of abstinence _____

Dates _____

Medical problems _____

_____

Physician _____ Phone _____

Medications _____

_____

Previously diagnosed psychiatric problems _____

_____

Dates _____

Suicide attempts or threats

_____

History of violence toward others

_____

Present legal problems

_____

Past legal problems

_____

Drugs used:

- Alcohol: Type(s) _____
  How often_____ How much _____
- Street drugs: Type(s) _____
  How often_____ How much _____
- Mood-altering prescription drugs: Type(s) _____

  _____

  How often_____ How much _____

- Inhalants: Type(s) _____
  How often_____ How much _____
- Other(s): Type(s) _____
  How often_____ How much _____

Consequences related to alcohol or other drug use:

- Job _____
- Relationships _____
- Divorce/separation _____
- Family _____
- Finances _____
- Legal _____
- Isolation _____
- Violence _____
- Dishonesty _____
- Concealing use _____
- Blackouts _____
- Drunken driving _____
- Mood swings _____
- Other _____

Other significant information: _____
_____
_____
_____
_____
_____

The Checklist

Preparation Is the Key to a Good Intervention

This checklist is designed to be used as an accompaniment to the book. Don't plan an intervention using the checklist alone.

- ☐ Bring together three to eight people who are important to the alcoholic and are willing to learn how to help.
- ☐ Read this book in its entirety for a precise education on how to motivate an addicted loved one to accept help.
- ☐ Set up a planning meeting to discuss moving forward with the intervention.
- ☐ Use the planner to record and organize information.
- ☐ Choose a detail person.
- ☐ Choose a team chairperson.
- ☐ Discuss the importance of not alerting the alcoholic to the intervention plans.
- ☐ List ways you've tried to help the alcoholic that may have actually enabled the addiction.
- ☐ Put in writing all the negative consequences caused by the addiction problem.
- ☐ Write a one- to two-page letter to the alcoholic.
- ☐ Read your letters to each other, editing out anger, blame, and judgment.

☐ Determine bottom lines, and write them down on a separate page.

☐ Test each other's willingness to follow through with the bottom lines.

☐ Identify financial resources for covering treatment costs.

☐ Evaluate treatment centers.

☐ Set a date, time, and place for the rehearsal and the intervention.

☐ Choose a treatment center, answer its pre-intake questions, and make an appointment for admission.

☐ Make airline reservations if the treatment center is out of state.

☐ Create a plan likely to guarantee the alcoholic's presence at the intervention.

☐ Identify objections the alcoholic may use to avoid or postpone treatment, then formulate your answers.

☐ Pack a suitcase using the guidelines provided by the treatment staff.

☐ Determine who should drive the alcoholic from the intervention to the treatment center.

☐ Compile a list of all prescribed medications the alcoholic is presently using.

☐ Rehearse the intervention
    ☐ Decide where each person will sit, including the alcoholic.
    ☐ Discuss the order in which you'll read your letters.
    ☐ Find a discreet place to park your cars.
    ☐ Script the chairman's introduction and closing statement.
    ☐ Review objections and answers.

☐ Call and confirm the admissions appointment at the treatment center.

☐ Rehearse the intervention exactly as you'll do the real thing.

☐ Plan to arrive at the intervention location thirty minutes before the alcoholic is expected to be there.

☐ If the intervention is taking place at the alcoholic's home, arrive as a complete group.

☐ After the intervention, call the admissions staff and let them know whether the alcoholic has agreed to treatment.

☐ Collect all letters and send them to the alcoholic's treatment counselor.

☐ Sign up for the family program.

☐ Locate an Al-Anon or Family Anonymous meeting near your home or office.

☐ Review resources in the appendix.

Enabling Behaviors

Out of love and fear, we do all sorts of things to protect our alcoholics. Most of the things we do, however, actually help the addiction instead. As a result, the addiction flourishes, and our loved ones get sicker. This is called enabling. Discover ways you've enabled the addiction and check all the behaviors you can recognize in yourself:

- ☐ Give or lend money
- ☐ Provide a place to live
- ☐ Clean up after messes
- ☐ Supply a car
- ☐ Bail out of jail
- ☐ Lie to cover up problems
- ☐ Deny the addiction to others
- ☐ Ignore or laugh at the problem
- ☐ Argue, plead, beg, threaten, placate, or bargain
- ☐ Put yourself in jeopardy
- ☐ Leave minor children alone with the alcoholic
- ☐ Take over responsibilities
- ☐ Protect from negative consequences
- ☐ Avoid social functions

☐ Offer a job

☐ Pay for school

☐ Pay for alcohol or other drug use

☐ Others _____

_____

_____

_____

_____

Evaluating Treatment Centers

Questions to Ask

In the planner you listed possible treatment center choices. Before deciding which you will use, learn about its program. Ask a qualified staff member the following questions:

- Is the treatment program based on the *Twelve Steps of Alcoholics Anonymous? The Twelve Steps are the most effective way to achieve long-term, contented sobriety.*
- Is the addiction to alcohol or other drugs treated as a primary disease? *Watch out for treatment centers approaching addiction as a secondary issue. In other words, they see addiction as a symptom of another problem and believe that fixing that problem makes the addiction go away. The opposite is true. We must treat the addiction first, before we can solve other problems.*
- Is complete abstinence of all mood-altering substances, including alcohol, the treatment goal? *Moderation programs have sprung up around the country with the goal of teaching people to drink moderately. People who are alcoholic cannot successfully use any amount of alcohol or other drugs. People who are addicted to prescription or illegal drugs cannot use alcohol.*

- Is inpatient, residential care available? *After an intervention, we prefer the support and concentration of residential care, at least initially. However, you may find that your insurance or other funding sources will only pay for outpatient care.*

- Does the counseling staff consult with the family throughout the treatment process? *Counselors and family members share important information about the alcoholic's history, progress in treatment, and aftercare plans. If the alcoholic refuses to sign a release form, The Federal Law on Confidentiality prevents counselors from speaking to family members.*

- Does the center provide Alcoholics Anonymous meetings during the treatment stay? *Ongoing Alcoholics Anonymous attendance is key to long-term sobriety. When alcoholics are introduced to Alcoholics Anonymous in treatment, they are more likely to continue to attend once discharged from treatment.*

- Is a family program available? *Is there an additional charge for this service? Attending a family program is an essential part of the family's recovery and supports the addicted person's recovery.*

- Can the program provide services for special needs the addicted person may have? *If the alcoholic has problems, such as illiteracy, hearing loss, limited mobility, or dual diagnosis, will the facility offer the appropriate services so these problems will not block treatment? If the patient is an older adult or an adolescent, is the program designed to meet his or her special needs?*

- If the alcoholic wants to leave treatment early, does the staff use conflict resolution to challenge the patient to stay? *As a result of denial, some patients decide to leave treatment against medical advice. Conflict resolution works very well in these cases.*

- Is an aftercare group available? *Aftercare groups usually meet one night a week and provide support during the transition between treatment and Alcoholics Anonymous or Narcotics Anonymous.*

- What percentage of the counseling staff is recovering in a Twelve Step program? *Counselors working their own Twelve Step programs—Al-Anon, Alcoholics Anonymous, Narcotics Anonymous, or any of the other programs—are most effective in helping alcoholics and addicts.*

- What percentage of the counseling staff is certified in addiction counseling? *Treating addiction requires very specific knowledge and skills. Look for a high percentage of certified addiction counselors.*

- Is there a medical doctor on staff and a detox unit? *If not, ask who they recommend for medical detox.*

- Is there a psychiatrist or psychologist on staff? *This is important if the alcoholic has mental health problems not caused by the addiction.*

Notes: _____

_____

_____

_____

_____

_____

_____

Objections and Answers

Working as a group, we prepare for all the possible objections the alcoholic might use to avoid accepting help. When writing your responses, keep them short and to the point. Below are some examples. Objections typically fall into the following five categories:

1. Work:

Objection: "I have to go to work. I'll lose my job if I don't."
Response: "We've contacted your Employee Assistance Program, and they've informed us that the company has a policy to support your decision to get help. They gave us a number for you to call when you get into treatment, and they will handle everything confidentially."

Objection: "I can't take time off right now, but give me a week to arrange it."
Response: "You don't need to worry. Everything is already arranged. Your job will be waiting for you once you've completed treatment."

Objection: "My boss can't do without me now. We're in the middle of an important project."
Response: "Your boss has written you a letter supporting treatment. He has asked us to read it to you."

Objection: "Work may say they're supportive, but they'll fire me anyway."

Response: "The Americans with Disabilities Act protects you from being fired. It is against the law for your employer to fire you for getting help for an alcohol or other drug problem."

Objection: "You don't know my boss. She'll find another reason to replace me."

Response: "It sounds like—if your boss has her way—you'll lose this job sooner or later anyway. Saving your life is more important then trying to save this job."

2. Money:

Objection: "I don't have any insurance. I can't afford to go into treatment."

Response: "We have taken care of everything. We've found an excellent low-cost (no-cost) treatment center." *or* "Your life is very important to us. We are taking care of all treatment costs."

Objection: "I'll lose my apartment if I can't pay the rent."

Response: "Your life is more important than your apartment. You can always find another place to live." *or* "We talked to your landlord and he's worked things out with a payment arrangement." *or* "As a family, we've pooled our resources and have enough money to cover your rent and utilities while you're in treatment."

3. Children:

Objection: "I can't go to treatment because I have to take care of my kids."

Response: "Your sister is going to take care of your children while you are in treatment."

Objection: "I couldn't leave my children like that. They need me."

Response: "Your children need a sober mother (father). Your alcohol problem is creating problems for them. Getting treatment is the best thing you can do for your children."

4. Social Obligations:

When an upcoming once-in-a-lifetime event is the objection, such as a wedding, graduation, or baptism, determine if intervening after the event is a better way to go. However, if the alcoholic or addict is very sick, in big trouble, or at high risk for imminent disaster, it could be too risky to wait. If you are in this difficult situation, consult with a professional interventionist.
Objection: "I can't go now. I'll miss Jenny and Dave's wedding."
Response: "You need help now. Jenny and Dave are very worried about you. They want you to know that the best wedding gift you can give them is going in for help today."

5. Denial:

Objection: "I can handle this on my own. I don't need help."
Response: "You've tried to control your drinking before. We now know that this is a disease and willpower doesn't work. We've learned that you need a specific kind of help in order to recover."
Objection: "Joe's been out drinking with me many times. Why is everybody singling me out?"
Response: "Today we're talking about your relationship with alcohol and what is happening to you."
Objection: "I don't drink every night. I mostly drink on weekends."
Response: "It is not about how much you drink or when you drink, but what happens to you when you drink."
Objection: "I'm not hurting anyone. It's none of your business."
Response: "You may not know it, but we are all very affected by your drinking. The whole family is suffering. Addiction is a family disease."

Bottom Lines

If you think you don't have a bottom line, go back and review ways you've enabled the addiction. Each of our enabling behaviors can be turned into a bottom line. The following examples will help you brainstorm.

"I will no longer give you money."

"I will not pay your mortgage from now on."

"If you do not accept help for your drug problem, you can no longer live in my home."

"I'm taking the car keys away until you get help for your alcohol problem."

"I'm not a liar, so I will no longer lie to people about your addiction problem."

"I've pretended not to notice your problem in the past. From now on, if you come over when you are high, I'm not going to let you in the house."

"The next time I see you get in the car to drive intoxicated, I will call the police."

"I won't listen to your problems until you get help for your number-one problem—alcohol and other drugs."

"I will no longer ride with you or socialize with you when you are drunk."

"Until you get into recovery, I cannot let my children spend time with you."

"I will no longer pick up your slack at work. When you don't get your work done, you'll have to explain to the boss."

"I'm not going to tell your boss you have the flu when you have a hangover."

"I will not invite you to family get-togethers until you get help for your drug problem."

"You can no longer work for me unless you complete treatment and stay sober."

"Your mom and I will quit paying your school expenses until you get help."

"If you don't get help on your own, we will have you court ordered into treatment."

The bottom line is not a punishment. It's a decision we make *not* to support the addiction and to take care of ourselves. For the alcoholic, the bottom line is a natural consequence of deciding to stay in the disease of addiction. Below, write three of your own bottom lines: _____

_____

_____

_____

_____

_____

_____

_____

Self-Quizzes

Families sometimes feel unsure about how to assess a loved one's problem. On the following pages you'll find five self-quizzes. They are designed to help you think about the possible chemical dependency of a loved one and how it has affected you. These quizzes are not scientific diagnostic tools. Some questions may carry more weight than others. They don't prove someone does or doesn't have a problem. You must rely on your discretion and common sense when evaluating the results.

These quizzes are *not* meant to be used as "evidence" to present to the chemically dependent person. *Do not bring any of these quizzes to the alcoholic or addict as proof or confirmation of addiction.* This would be an inappropriate way to discuss the problem and may cause angry and resentful reactions from the addict.

Quiz: Is a Family Member Chemically Dependent?

To determine whether or not an alcohol or drug problem is affecting your family, ask yourself the following questions:

- ☐ Does someone in your family undergo personality changes when he or she uses alcohol or other drugs?
- ☐ Are you sometimes anxious before holidays or special occasions because you are worried that he or she may disrupt it by getting high or drunk?
- ☐ Have you ever found it necessary to lie to employers, relatives, or friends to hide his or her alcohol or drug use?
- ☐ Have you ever hidden car keys, thrown out the alcohol or drugs, or used other methods to attempt to control his or her use?
- ☐ Have you ever felt embarrassed or felt the need to apologize for his or her actions?
- ☐ Have you ever asked him or her to stop or cut down on his or her use of alcohol or other drugs?
- ☐ Has he or she ever promised to stop using alcohol or other drugs without success?
- ☐ Has he or she ever failed to remember what occurred during a period of alcohol and/or drug use?
- ☐ Does he or she avoid social situations where alcohol and/or drugs will not be available?
- ☐ Does he or she have periods of remorse after periods of use and does he or she apologize for his or her behavior?

☐ Does he or she justify his or her use by blaming a stressful lifestyle or difficult emotional situations?

☐ Do other family members fear or avoid this person after he or she has been using alcohol or other drugs?

☐ Has another person expressed concern about his or her drinking or drug use?

☐ Has he or she ever made promises that he or she did not keep because of drinking or drug use?

☐ Has his or her reaction to a given amount of alcohol or other drugs changed?

☐ Does he or she deny a drinking problem because he or she drinks only wine or beer?

☐ Do you find yourself avoiding social situations that include alcohol or other drugs?

If you answered "yes" to any of the above questions, there is a possibility that someone in your family is developing a problem with alcohol or other drugs. If you answered "yes" to two or more, chemical use is probably causing serious problems in your family.

Reprinted with permission of Substance Abuse Community Council of Grosse Pointe from the pamphlet "How Do I Know? Where Do I Go?"

Quiz: Signs of Alcoholism and Drug Abuse in Older People

The signs of alcoholism and drug addiction can be different in adults fifty-five years old and over than in younger people. They often drink alone at home so no one notices the severity of the problem. Many older adults are retired, so they don't have work-related problems due to their chemical dependency. They drive less, so there's less opportunity for them to get arrested for driving under the influence.

The following signs of an alcohol or other drug problem are typical in the older adult:

- ☐ Prefers attending a lot of events where drinking is accepted, such as luncheons, "happy hours," and parties
- ☐ Drinks in solitary, hidden away
- ☐ Makes a ritual of having drinks before, with, or after dinner, and becomes annoyed when this ritual is disturbed
- ☐ Loses interest in activities and hobbies that used to bring pleasure
- ☐ Drinks in spite of warning labels on prescription drugs
- ☐ Always has bottles of tranquilizers on hand and takes them at the slightest sign of disturbance
- ☐ Is often intoxicated or slightly tipsy, and sometimes has slurred speech

☐ Disposes of large volumes of empty beer and liquor bottles and seems secretive about it

☐ Often has the smell of liquor on his or her breath or mouthwash to disguise it

☐ Is neglecting personal appearance and gaining or losing weight

☐ Complains of constant sleeplessness, loss of appetite, or chronic health complaints that seem to have no physical cause

☐ Has unexplained burns or bruises and tries to hide them

☐ Seems more depressed or hostile than usual

☐ Can't handle routine chores and paperwork without making mistakes

☐ Has irrational or undefined fears or delusions, or seems under unusual stress

☐ Seems to be losing his or her memory

Many of the symptoms listed above are attributed to other diseases or are considered part of the aging process. However, many older people find that once they achieve sobriety, these symptoms disappear.

Reprinted from the pamphlet "How to Talk to an Older Person Who Has a Problem with Alcohol or Medications," published by Hazelden. Reprinted by permission of Hazelden. To obtain copies of the pamphlet, call 800-I-DO-CARE.

Quiz: Is Our Teen Chemically Dependent?

Some symptoms of teen alcohol and drug abuse are not clear cut. Many of the signs can be confused with normal adolescent behavior or with health dysfunction. However, it is critical to be alert and to know that a combination of the following characteristics may be cause for concern.

☐ Has your child's personality changed noticeably? Does he or she have sudden mood swings and unpredictable behavior?

☐ Does your child seem to be losing old friends and spending time with a new group about whom you know little or who are known as a party bunch?

☐ Is your child unable to account for large sums of his or her money, or have you had objects or money mysteriously disappearing from your home?

☐ Does your child defend his or her right to drink?

☐ Is your child reluctant to talk about alcohol or other drugs?

☐ Does your child drive irresponsibly?

☐ Does your child lie about drug and alcohol use as well as other activities?

☐ Have you ever found drug paraphernalia (rolling papers, baggies, small spoons, roach clips, capsules), bottles, or beer cans in his or her room? Did your child explain it away when confronted?

☐ Has your child lost interest in his or her physical appearance?

☐ Has your child admitted to trying alcohol or other drugs "just once" while denying any regular use?

☐ Are you hearing rumors about your child's partying, goofing off, or drinking?

☐ Has your child been cutting classes?

☐ Do you as parents conceal from each other information about your child's behavior?

☐ Is your child suddenly less responsive? Is she or he losing interest in school work, athletics, extracurricular activities, family, job, and/or other previous interests? Are grades dropping (not necessarily from A's to D's but from B's to C's)?

☐ Do you detect any of these physical symptoms: excessive fatigue, disturbed sleep patterns, chronic cough, chest pains, "allergy" symptoms, vomiting, loss of appetite, unusual craving for sweets, red eyes, dilation of pupils?

☐ Have your child's relationships with other family members deteriorated?

☐ Are there signs of apparent emotional or psychological problems such as depression, loneliness, paranoia, or withdrawal?

If you answered "yes" to any two of the above questions, there is a possibility that your teen is developing a problem with alcohol or other drugs. If you answered "yes" to three or more questions, chemical use is probably causing serious problems in your family.

Reprinted with permission of Substance Abuse Community Council of Grosse Pointe from the pamphlet "How Do I Know? Where Do I Go?"

Quiz: Signs of Inhalant Use

Evaluate the following signs and symptoms of inhalant use based on the number of different signs observed, their frequency, and overall behavior.

- ☐ Does the child have a red, runny nose or eyes?
- ☐ Have you noticed excessive or inappropriate laughter?
- ☐ Are the eyes glassy? Are the pupils dilated or constricted?
- ☐ Is the child sweating for no obvious reason?
- ☐ Have you noticed paranoia, irritability, excitability, or anxiety?
- ☐ Are there times when the child speaks in a nonsensical way?
- ☐ Has the child withdrawn from old friends?
- ☐ Is the child hanging around a new crowd? Do you have concerns about him or her? Does the child keep them away from the family?
- ☐ Is the child exhibiting apathy to things he or she used to care about?
- ☐ Have you found plastic bags, rags, or cotton with a chemical odor?
- ☐ Have you seen correction fluid, paint, or stains on the child's face, fingers, or clothing?
- ☐ Have you found household solvents, cleaners, or adhesives hidden in the child's room?

☐ Are there spots or sores around the mouth?

☐ Have you ever detected a chemical odor to the child's breath?

☐ Has the child appeared dazed or dizzy?

☐ Has the child's appetite decreased? Does he or she complain of nausea?

If you come upon your child or teen in the act of sniffing inhalants, remain calm. Excitement or outrage may cause someone under the influence of inhalants to become violent, start hallucinating, or suffer heart problems, which can lead to death. Ventilate the room and call 911. If the child stops breathing, administer CPR.

Sudden Sniffing Death Syndrome can happen to first-time users as well as chronic users. Go to the National Inhalant Prevention Coalition's Web site at **www.inhalants.org** for more information on inhalant abuse.

Adapted from the National Inhalant Prevention Coalition's Web site.

Quiz: Are You Troubled by Someone's Drinking?

This following questionnaire was designed by Al-Anon to help you decide whether Al-Anon is right for you. As you take this quiz, keep in mind that you may have been affected by a parent's drinking when you were a child. Although Al-Anon does not provide guidelines on how to evaluate your answers to this quiz, we suggest you attend Al-Anon if you answer "yes" to two or more questions.

☐ Do you worry about how much someone drinks?

☐ Do you have money problems because of someone else's drinking?

☐ Do you tell lies to cover up for someone else's drinking?

☐ Do you feel if the drinker loved you, he or she would stop drinking to please you?

☐ Do you blame the drinker's behavior on his or her companions?

☐ Are plans frequently upset or canceled or meals delayed because of the drinker?

☐ Do you make threats, such as, "If you don't stop drinking, I'll leave you"?

☐ Do you secretly try to smell the drinker's breath?

☐ Are you afraid to upset someone for fear it will set off a drinking bout?

☐ Have you been hurt or embarrassed by a drinker's behavior?

- [ ] Are holidays and gatherings spoiled because of drinking?
- [ ] Have you considered calling the police for help, for fear of abuse?
- [ ] Do you search for hidden alcohol?
- [ ] Do you often ride in a car with a driver who has been drinking?
- [ ] Have you refused social invitations out of fear or anxiety?
- [ ] Do you sometimes feel like a failure when you think of the lengths you have gone to to protect the drinker?
- [ ] Do you think that if the drinker stopped drinking, your other problems would be solved?
- [ ] Do you ever threaten to hurt yourself to scare the drinker?
- [ ] Do you feel angry, confused, or depressed most of the time?
- [ ] Do you feel there is no one who understands your problems?

From "Are You Troubled by Someone's Drinking?" copyright 1980, by Al-Anon Family Group Headquarters, Inc. Reprinted by permission of Al-Anon Family Group Headquarters, Inc.

THE JELLINEK CURVE

Addiction and Recovery

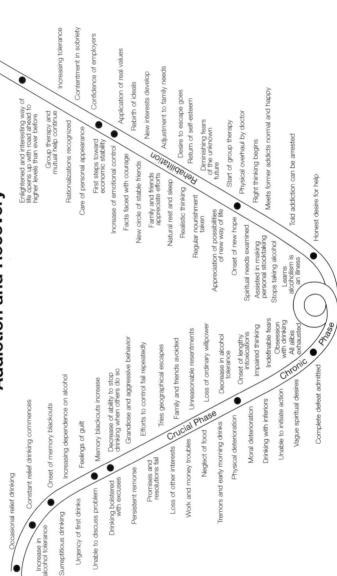

Occasional relief drinking

Increase in alcohol tolerance

Constant relief drinking commences

Surreptitious drinking

Onset of memory blackouts

Urgency of first drinks

Increasing dependence on alcohol

Unable to discuss problem

Feelings of guilt

Memory blackouts increase

Drinking bolstered with excuses

Decrease of ability to stop drinking when others do so

Persistent remorse

Grandiose and aggressive behavior

Promises and resolutions fail

Efforts to control fail repeatedly

Loss of other interests

Tries geographical escapes

Work and money troubles

Family and friends avoided

Unreasonable resentments

Neglect of food

Loss of ordinary willpower

Tremors and early morning drinks

Decrease in alcohol tolerance

Physical deterioration

Onset of lengthy intoxications

Moral deterioration

Impaired thinking

Drinking with inferiors

Indefinable fears

Unable to initiate action

Obsession with drinking

Vague spiritual desires

All alibis exhausted

Complete defeat admitted

Crucial Phase

Chronic Phase

Obsessive drinking continues in vicious circles

Learns alcoholism is an illness

Stops taking alcohol

Assisted in making personal stocktaking

Spiritual needs examined

Onset of new hope

Appreciation of possibilities of new way of life

Regular nourishment taken

Realistic thinking

Natural rest and sleep

Family and friends appreciate efforts

New circle of stable friends

Facts faced with courage

Increase of emotional control

First steps toward economic stability

Care of personal appearance

Rationalizations recognized

Group therapy and mutual help continue

Enlightened and interesting way of life opens up with road ahead to higher levels than ever before

Increasing tolerance

Contentment in sobriety

Confidence of employers

Application of real values

Rebirth of ideals

New interests develop

Adjustment to family needs

Desire to escape goes

Return of self-esteem

Diminishing fears of the unknown future

Start of group therapy

Physical overhaul by doctor

Right thinking begins

Meets former addicts normal and happy

Told addiction can be arrested

Honest desire for help

Rehabilitation

APPENDIXES

Appendix A

Twelve Steps of Alcoholics Anonymous*

1. We admitted we were powerless over alcohol—that our lives had become unmanageable.

2. Came to believe that a Power greater than ourselves could restore us to sanity.

3. Made a decision to turn our will and our lives over to the care of God *as we understood Him.*

4. Made a searching and fearless moral inventory of ourselves.

5. Admitted to God, to ourselves, and to another human being the exact nature of our wrongs.

6. Were entirely ready to have God remove all these defects of character.

7. Humbly asked Him to remove our shortcomings.

8. Made a list of all persons we had harmed, and became willing to make amends to them all.

9. Made direct amends to such people wherever possible, except when to do so would injure them or others.

10. Continued to take personal inventory and when we were wrong promptly admitted it.

---

* The Twelve Steps of AA are taken from *Alcoholics Anonymous,* 3d ed., published by AA World Services, Inc., New York, N.Y., 59–60. Reprinted with permission of AA World Services, Inc. (See author's note on copyright page.)

11. Sought through prayer and meditation to improve our conscious contact with God *as we understood Him,* praying only for knowledge of His will for us and the power to carry that out.

12. Having had a spiritual awakening as the result of these steps, we tried to carry this message to alcoholics, and to practice these principles in all our affairs.

Appendix B

Resources

Web Sites

- National Association for Children of Alcoholics: www.health.org/nacoa/

- Christians in Recovery: **www.christians-in-recovery.com**

- Hazelden Foundation: **www.hazelden.org**

- The Intervention Resource Center: **www.interventioninfo.org**

- Jewish Alcoholics, Chemically Dependent Persons and Significant Others: **www.jacsweb.org**

- National Council on Alcoholism and Other Drug Dependence: **www.ncadd.org**

- National Inhalant Prevention Coalition: **www.inhalants.org**

- National Institute on Alcohol Abuse and Alcoholism: **www.niaaa.nih.giv**

- Office of National Drug Control Policy: **www.whitehousedrugpolicy.gov**

- The Recovery Network: **www.recoverynetwork.com**

- Recovery Online: **www.onlinerecovery.org**

- Terry McGovern Foundation: **www.terrymcgovern.org**

Books and Publications

- Wegsheider Cruse, Sharon. *Another Chance: Hope and Health for the Alcoholic Family*. Science and Behavior Books, 1989. Describes the family disease of alcoholism and the roles family members subconsciously adopt to cope with the problem.

- Ketcham, Kathy, et al. *Beyond the Influence: Understanding and Defeating Alcoholism*. Bantam Doubleday Dell, 2000. Clearly explains the neurochemical nature of the disease of alcoholism and reveals why some people drink addictively while others don't. Explains what needs to be done to treat alcoholism.

- Hammond, Robert L., ed. *The Bottom Line on Alcohol in Society*. Alcohol Research Information Service. A quarterly journal that collects and correlates information from a wide range of sources. Reports information not always found in mainstream media. For subscription information, call (517)485- 9900 or fax (517)485-1928.

- Larsen, Earnie. *From Anger to Forgiveness*. Hazelden, 1992. A practical guide to breaking the negative power of anger and achieving reconciliation.

- Various authors. *Hazelden Meditation Series*. Hazelden. The books in this series have guided millions of recovering people, their families, and those looking for spiritual growth. Titles include: *Each Day a New Beginning: Daily Meditations for Women; Days of Healing, Days of Joy; In God's Care: Daily Meditations on Spirituality in Recovery*.

- Gorski, Terence T. *Passages through Recovery: An Action Plan for Preventing Relapse*. Hazelden, 1997.

- Various authors. *Talk, Trust, and Feel: Keeping Codependency Out of Your Life*. Hazelden, 1991. Offers inspiring perspectives on the relationship problem called codependency.

Twelve Step Organizations

Al-Anon/Alateen Family Group, (888)4AL-ANON. Web site: **www.al-anon.org**. Helps families and friends of alcoholics recover from the effects of living with the problem drinking of a relative or friend. Alateen is a similar program for youth. Call for meetings in the United States and Canada.

Alcoholics Anonymous, (212)870-3400. Web site: **www.alcoholics-anony-mous.org.** A fellowship of men and women who have had a drinking problem. It is nonprofessional, self-supporting, nondenominational, multiracial, apolitical, and available most places.

Cocaine Anonymous, (310)559-5833. **Web site: www.ca.org.** Adapted from the Alcoholics Anonymous program, the only requirement for membership is the desire to stop using cocaine and all other mood-altering substances.

Debtors Anonymous, (781)453-2743. Web site: **www.debtorsanony-mous.org.** The goal is to live without incurring any unsecured debt and to help other compulsive debtors achieve solvency.

Families Anonymous, (800)736-9805. Web site: **www.familiesanony-mous.org.** A program for family members and friends concerned about someone's current, suspected, or past drug, alcohol, or related behavioral problems. Call for meetings in the United States and Canada.

Gamblers Anonymous, (213)386-8789. Web site: **www.gamblersanony-mous.org.** A fellowship of men and women who share their experience, strength, and hope with each other so that they may solve their common problem of gambling and help others.

Gam-Anon, (718)352-1671. Web site: **www.gam-anon.org.** Composed of men and women who are husbands, wives, relatives, or close friends of compulsive gamblers.

Nar-Anon Family Groups, (310)547-5800. For friends and relatives of people addicted to illegal drugs or narcotics, and the special problems that result from those addictions. Consult your phone book for a local listing.

Narcotics Anonymous, (818)773-9999. Web site: **www.na.org.** A program that reaches out to people addicted to illegal drugs or narcotics.

Overeaters Anonymous, (505)891-2664. Web site: **www.overeatersanony-mous.org.** A program for individuals recovering from compulsive overeating.

S-Anon International Family Groups, (615)833-3152. Web site: **www.sanon.org.** Support for people living with the problem of a friend or relative's sexaholism.

Sex Addicts Anonymous, (612)339-0217. Web site: **www.sexaa.org.** Reaches out to people who want to avoid compulsive and destructive sexual behaviors.

Sexaholics Anonymous, (615)331-6230. Web site: **www.sa.org.** The program defines sexual sobriety as no sex with self and no sex outside of marriage.

ALCOHOL AND DRUG TREATMENT CENTERS FOR SPECIAL POPULATIONS

OLDER ADULT PROGRAMS, AGES FIFTY-FIVE AND OLDER:

Hanley-Hazelden Older Adult Program, 5200 East Avenue, West Palm Beach, FL 33407; (800)444-7008. Web site: **www.hazelden.org.** A treatment program for older adults addicted to alcohol or prescription drugs. Residential and day programs are available. The facility includes a serenity garden and a chapel.

Hopedale Hall, 107 Tremont Street, P.O. Box 267, Hopedale, IL 61747; (800)344-0824. Web site: **www.hmc.net.** A sixty-day residential, Twelve Step rehabilitation program for alcoholics and addicts more than fifty years old. Special facilities and programs are available for those with physical impairments and impaired cognitive/intellectual memory skills.

YOUTH PROGRAMS:

Brighton Hospital Adolescent Treatment Center, 12851 East Grand River, Brighton, MI 48116; (888)215-2700. Web site: **www.brightonhospital.org.** A secure facility designed to address adolescent addiction and dual diagnosis. Includes a gymnasium, weight room, art room, and computer-equipped classroom with certified instructors. Accepts male and female youth ages twelve to eighteen.

Caron Adolescent Center, Galen Hall Road, Box A, Wernersville, PA 19565; (800)678-2332. Web site: **www.caron.org.** A treatment program designed for youth ages twelve to nineteen. Situated in a mountain setting, the program offers group, individual, and family therapy. An on-site teaching staff provides alternative classroom instruction and contact with the patient's home school district. Caron is a gender-separate program and offers an extended care program for adolescents who need additional support after completing treatment.

Hazelden Center for Youth and Families, 11505 36th Avenue North, Plymouth, MN 55441; (800)257-7810. Web site: **www.hazelden.org.** Residential and outpatient treatment for youth ages fourteen to twenty-five. Other services include extended care, parent education, and outpatient counseling clinic.

Sundown M Youth Treatment Center, P.O. Box 217, Selah, WA 98942; (800)326-7444. Web site: **www.sundown.org.** Provides a program with a minimum twenty-eight-day stay. Accepts male and female youth, but treatment groups and living quarters are gender-specific with two separate wings. The school program is staffed by certified teachers. Grades 4 through 12 are offered. Patients work on assignments from their home schools. Treatment includes a two-phase family counseling program.

Wilderness Treatment Center, 200 Hubbart Dam Road, Marion, MT 59925; John Brekke, Director; (406)854-2832. Web site: **www.wildernessaltschool.com.** The sixty-day treatment program begins with thirty days of traditional Twelve Step–based treatment. The second month includes a sixteen- to twenty-one-day-long, Outward Bound–style trip. Accepts males ages fourteen to twenty.

HOMOSEXUAL PROGRAMS:

Pride Institute, 168 5th Ave., Suite 4S, New York, NY 10010; (800)54-PRIDE. Web site: **Pride-Institute.com.** Provides treatment for alcohol and other drug addictions for the gay, lesbian, bisexual, and transgender communities. Call to inquire about program locations nationwide.

DUAL DIAGNOSIS:

Advanced Recovery Center (ARC), 1300 Park of Commerce Blvd., #200, Delray Beach, FL 33445; (877)ARC-HOPE. Treats chemically dependent men and women, ages eighteen and older, who require additional treatment to address underlying psychiatric issues including depression, bipolar disorder, attention deficit disorder, personality disorders, obsessive-compulsive disorder, eating disorders, post-traumatic stress disorder, and chronic addictions relapse. ARC requires daily involvement in a Twelve Step program. Men and women are housed separately in well-appointed apartments one mile from the beach. They have access to a health and fitness center.

Help Lines and Links

Hazelden Foundation. (800)257-7800. This is a help line for people seeking guidance for themselves or loved ones. Hours: every day, 8:00 A.M.–8:30 P.M. CST.

National Clearinghouse for Alcohol and Drug Information. English: (800)729-6686. Hablamos Espanol: (877)767-8432. TDD: (800)487-4889. Information specialists are trained to answer questions about alcohol and substance abuse prevention, intervention, and treatment. They are also trained to handle crisis telephone calls. Hours: Monday through Friday, 8:00 A.M.–7:00 P.M. EST.

National Council on Alcoholism and Drug Dependence. (800)NCA-CALL. Twenty-four-hour referral to local NCADD affiliates who can provide information and referrals to services in callers' local areas.

National Institute on Drug Abuse. (800)662-HELP. Provides printed drug-related information and helps locate treatment programs.

CyberSober.com, **www.cybersober.com.** Using the technology of MapQuest, this site generates maps and driving instructions to 133,000 Alcoholics Anonymous, Al-Anon, and other Twelve Step meetings. Other recovery-related information and on-line meetings are available. A membership fee is required for use of services.

Index

About the Authors

JEFF JAY began his career as an alcohol and drug counselor in 1986. Since then, he has worked as a supervisor, trainer, and program designer. He has also been seen on CNN and PBS and has had his work featured in *Parade* magazine, *USA Today,* and the *Washington Post.*

Jeff is now a professional interventionist, working with families and businesses on a national basis. He is a graduate of the University of Minnesota and a certified addictions professional. He lives with his wife Debra in Grosse Pointe Farms, Michigan. His personal recovery from alcohol and drug addiction dates from October 4, 1981.

DEBRA JAY is the coauthor of two Hazelden Guidebooks—*Love First: A New Approach to Intervention for Alcoholism and Drug Addiction* and *Aging and Addiction: Helping Older Adults Overcome Alcohol or Medication Dependence.*

She is in private practice as an interventionist specializing in chemically dependent older adults. She provides intervention training and consultation to families throughout the United States and Canada. Debra has also been writing a regular newspaper column on alcohol and drugs in society since 1996.

You can contact Jeff and Debra Jay through their
Web site at www.lovefirst.net.